THE PRIDE of CHICAGO

The White Sox's 2005 Championship Season

Sporting News
BOOKS

Book design: Bill Wilson

Cover design: Michael Behrens

Photo Editors: Michael McNamara, Sean Gallagher, Paul Nisely

Contributing writers: Chris DeLuca, Sean Deveney, Stan McNeal, John Rawlings, Ron Smith

Copy editors: Zach Bodendieck, Tom Dienhart, Joe Hoppel, Ron Smith

Page design and production: Bill Wilson, Bob Parajon

Prepress specialists: Steve Romer, Pamela Speh, Russ Carr, Vern Kasal

PHOTO CREDITS:

T = Top, B = Bottom, R = Right, L = Left, M = Middle

Jay Drowns/TSN: 2-3, 5, 7, 13(5), 14-15, 17, 19R(5), 20, 21, 22, 24, 29, 30, 31(2), 32(2), 33(2), 34-35(3), 36(3), 37, 38(2), 39(2), 40(3), 41, 43(6), 44-45(4), 46(2), 47, 48-49(2), 50(3), 51(2), 58L, 59B, 59T, 59TR, 60, 61(2), 62, 63(2), 64(3), 65L, 67(2), 68L, 69(3), 70(3), 71(4), 94, 96, 97(2), 98, 100(2), 101R, 102BL, 105(2), 108T, 111(2), 112T, 113BR, 116 (Garland, Springer, Wheeler, Politte, Cotts, Hermanson), 117 (Astacio, Vizcaino, Jenks, Rodriguez, Marte, Buehrle), 120R, 121(2), 124, 127, 128TL, 128TR, 130BL, 131TL, 131TR, 131MR, 132-133, 134L(3), 138-139, 140, 143

Robert Seale/TSN: Front cover, 99(2), 101T, 102T, 102R, 104(3), 106(2), 107, 108(3), 109B, 110(3), 112B(2), 113T, 113TR, 113M, 113BL, 114, 115, 116TL, 116 (Oswalt, Gallo, Lidge, Hernandez), 117 (Qualls), 118T, 119T, 120T, 120L, 125(2), 126T, 126MR, 126B, 128B, 130BR, 131B

Albert Dickson/TSN: 23, 25, 118B, 119B, 120B, 122(2), 123, 126ML, 129, 130T(3), 137, 144

John Cordes for TSN: 58R, 59M(2), 72, 73, 74(4), 75, 76, 77(3), 78, 79, 80(4), 81B, 81R, 82(2), 83(4), 84, 85(2), 86(2), 87(4), 88(2), 89(3), 90-91

Sporting News Archives: 65R

AP/Wide World Photos: 16L, 26, 66, Charles Rex Arbogast; 18, 135, Jeff Roberson; 27T, Brian Kersey; 27B, Nam Y. Huh; 42L, 42M, Steven Senne; 42B, 55T, 57L, Winslow Townson; 52-53, Elise Amendola; 54, 55B, 56, Charles Krupa; 57R, Stephan Savoia; 68R, Ann Heisenfelt; 81, Mark Terrill; 103, Morry Gash

Getty Images: Back cover, Tim Boyle; 95, Jonathan Daniel

Copyright © 2005 by The Sporting News, a division of Vulcan Sports Media, 10176 Corporate Square Drive, Suite 200, St. Louis, MO 63132. All rights reserved. No part of *The Pride of Chicago* may be reproduced or transmitted in any form or by any means, electronic or mechanical, including photocopy, recording or any other information storage and retrieval system now known or to be invented, without permission in writing from the publisher, except by a reviewer who wishes to quote brief passages in connection with a review written for inclusion in a magazine, newspaper or broadcast. The Sporting News is a federally registered trademark of Vulcan Sports Media, Inc. Visit our website at www.sportingnews.com.
ISBN: 0-89204-845-X

10 9 8 7 6 5 4 3 2 1

CONTENTS

Foreword by Ozzie Guillen 6

Past Champions 8

The Regular Season 12

The Division Series 42
    Game 1 44
    Game 2 48
    Game 3 52

The League Championship Series 58
    Game 1 60
    Game 2 66
    Game 3 72
    Game 4 78
    Game 5 84

The World Series 92
    Scene setter: Sox fans have baseball; Cubs fans have beer ... 94
    Game 1 98
    Game 2 106
    Game 3 114
    Game 4 122
    Closer: Good old country hardball 136

2005 Game-by-Game Log 138

FOREWORD

BY OZZIE GUILLEN

On the day we won the World Series, bringing a championship to Chicago for the first time in 88 years, my heart was pounding like crazy. I was nervous, just because I was so excited, saying to myself, "When is this moment going to happen? A lot of people are waiting for this moment." Then it happened. Those people don't have to wait anymore.

I played in Chicago for 13 years, and I know there are a lot of good fans there who deserve this. And there are a lot of other people who deserve this, who worked hard to make it happen, starting with the players. When they won it, and they started celebrating on the field, I thought, "I'm so glad to see my boys, my players, jumping back and forth and celebrating this." Because it was an amazing feeling seeing them jump like little kids.

Jerry Reinsdorf, too, deserves this. This is something he has wanted for years, the World Series trophy. He worked so hard in baseball, it's unbelievable. And Ken Williams, the general manager. He gave me the best guys he could, guys who would fight for me and this team. The unity of this team, it was great, and it starts with Jerry and Kenny.

I thought about other Latin players. Baseball honored Latin players this season, and it is a great feeling when people from another country make a tribute like that. It's a great thing to be recognized and appreciated for all the hard work the Latin players in this country have done.

As happy as I was to watch my players celebrate, to hug my kids in the dugout, to have fans celebrate in Chicago, I know they were going crazy in Venezuela. I wanted to be there to see it. I thought, finally, I did something nice to make Venezuela happy.

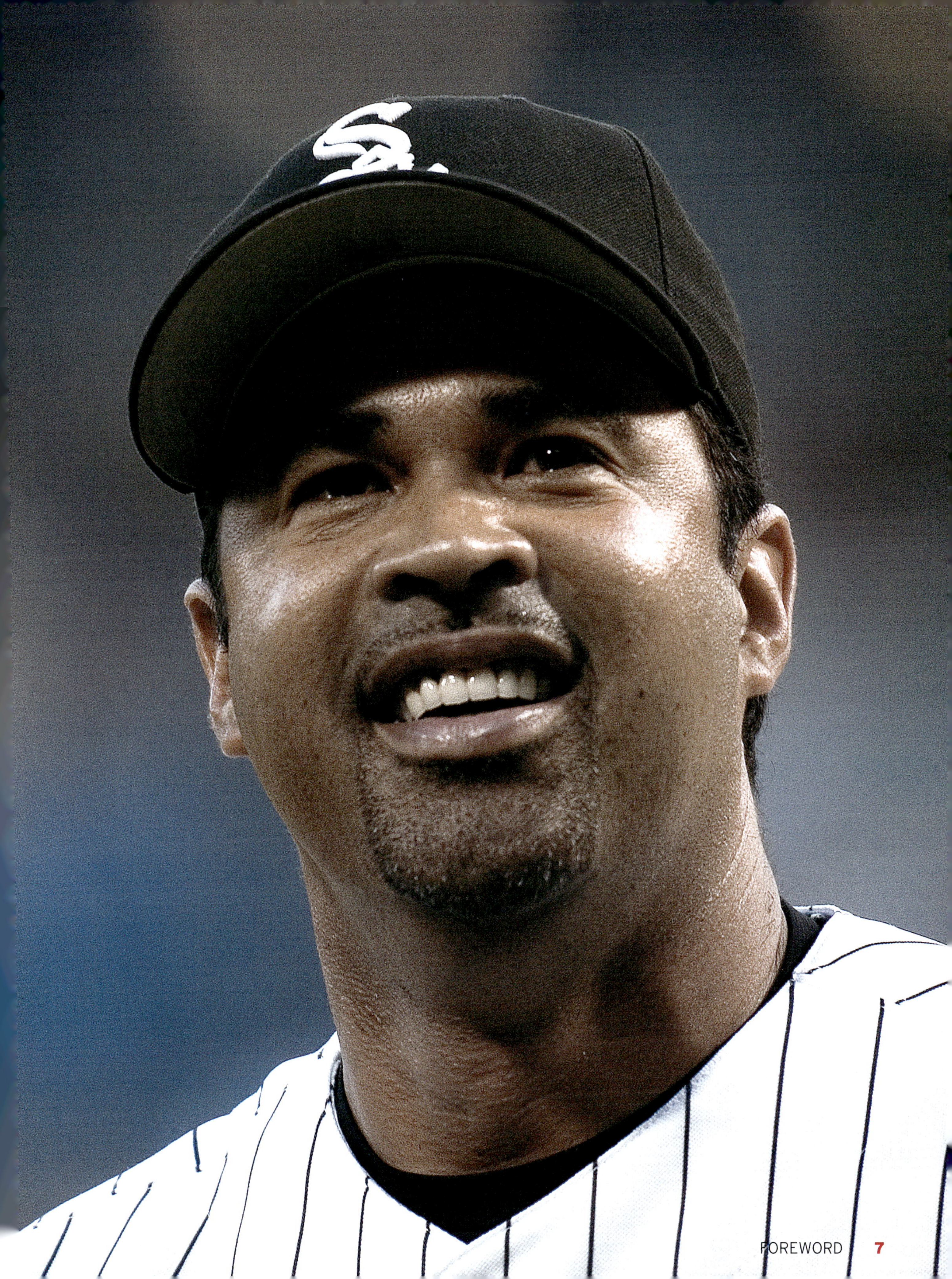

WORLD SERIES

1906

Baseball's third World Series was an all-Chicago extravaganza–and a classic mismatch. The Tinker-to-Evers-to-Chance Cubs had won a major league-record 116 games while posting a team ERA of 1.76; the "Hitless Wonder" White Sox had won 93 times with a collective team batting average of .228. The Cubs, it seemed, were destined for legendary acclaim.

But such White Sox players as Nick Altrock, Big Ed Walsh, Doc White, George Rohe, Frank Isbell and George Davis had other ideas. Walsh, the Sox's righthanded spitballer, won two games, Altrock and White won one apiece and Rohe, Isbell and Davis provided enough timely offense to help the Sox pull off a stunning six-game victory.

Manager Fielder Jones watched his White Sox stay even through four games, even though they managed only 11 hits and six runs. The four-hit pitching of Altrock gave the Sox a 2-1 win in the opener and, after a 7-1 Game 2 loss, the Sox prevailed 3-0 in Game 3 on Walsh's two-hit pitching and Rohe's bases-loaded triple.

Mordecai "Three Finger" Brown matched Walsh's two-hitter in Game 4, a 1-0 Cubs victory, but the White Sox bats suddenly came alive. Over the next two games, second baseman Isbell exploded for seven hits in 10 at-bats and shortstop Davis drove in six runs as the White Sox posted 8-6 and 8-3 wins that completed one of the great upsets in World Series history.

Chicago's 'Hitless Wonder' White Sox, with a lot of help from pitcher Ed Walsh (right) and George Rohe (far right), won a six-game World Series and bragging rights in 1906 when they upset the powerful Cubs.

THE White Sox of 1906, "The Hitless Wonders," world's champions. Upper row, left to right, Hart, E McFarland, Davis, Comiskey, Isbell, Sullivan, White. Middle row: Walsh, Smith, Roth, Hahn, Dundon Donohue, O'Neill, Tannehill, Rohe. Lower row: Towne, Altrock, Owen, Hallman, Dougherty, Jones, Fiene

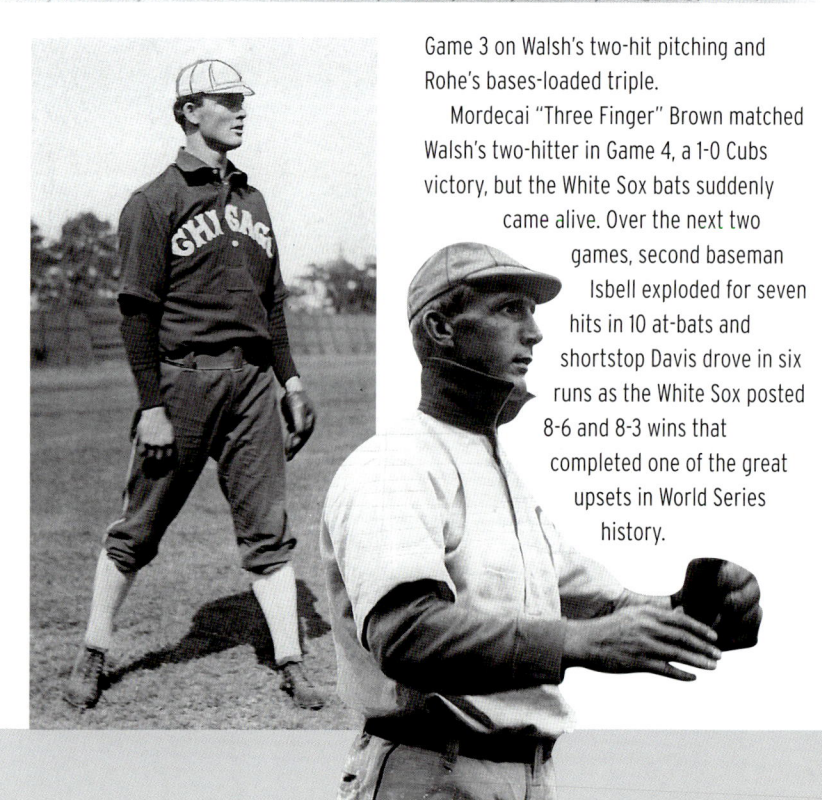

THE PRIDE OF CHICAGO

CHAMPIONS

1917

The White Sox, featuring all eight of the players who would later be banned for their roles in the infamous 1919 World Series fix, needed six games to dispatch John McGraw's New York Giants and capture their second fall classic championship.

This was a Series dominated by workhorse righthanders Red Faber, who pitched 27 innings in four games and recorded three victories, and Eddie Cicotte, who worked 23 innings and won once. Cicotte, who won 28 games in the regular season, got the Sox off to a good start with a 2-1 victory in Game 1 at Comiskey Park. Faber won Games 2 and 6 as a starter, Game 5 with two innings of relief. He also was the losing pitcher in New York's 5-0 win in Game 4.

The Giants contributed to their own downfall in the finale with a series of mistakes that led to a three-run Chicago fourth inning. Eddie Collins reached second base on a throwing error by third baseman Heinie Zimmerman and moved to third when right fielder Dave Robertson dropped Joe Jackson's fly ball. When Happy Felsch grounded back to Rube Benton, the Giants pitcher saw Collins break off third and threw behind him to Zimmerman, who ran Collins toward the plate.

The move backfired as Collins dashed past catcher Bill Rariden and outraced Zimmerman home. Jackson and Felsch later scored on Chick Gandil's single and Faber took care of the rest in a 4-2 Series-clinching win.

Red Faber (above) won three games for the White Sox in the 1917 World Series, the franchise's last championship before 2005. The most memorable play of the Series occurred in Game 6 when Giants third baseman Heinie Zimmerman, discovering too late his catcher was out of position, gave futile chase to Sox runner Eddie Collins, who slid home safely with the game's first run.

PAST CHAMPIONS 9

AMERICAN LEAGUE

Chicago's 1919 infield featured (left to right) Buck Weaver, Swede Risberg, Eddie Collins and Chick Gandil. All but Collins were banned from baseball. Also banned was slugging outfielder Joe Jackson (right).

1919

Chicago's third World Series appearance is remembered as one of the darkest chapters in baseball history. After the powerful Sox had fallen in eight games (the Series had just changed to a best-of-nine format) to the Cincinnati Reds, it was learned that some Chicago players had conspired with gamblers to throw the Series—a scandal that eventually led to the lifetime suspension of eight members of the team, including Shoeless Joe Jackson.

The "Black Sox" scandal claimed the careers of pitchers Eddie Cicotte and Lefty Williams, outfielders Jackson and Happy Felsch, first baseman Chick Gandil, shortstop Swede Risberg, third baseman Buck Weaver and reserve infielder Fred McMullin, all of whom were banned from baseball by commissioner Kenesaw Mountain Landis.

THE PRIDE OF CHICAGO

CHAMPIONS

1959

Chicago's last World Series representative before 2005 still is remembered affectionately as the "Go Go" Sox. Managed by Al Lopez and led by speedy shortstop Luis Aparicio and second baseman Nellie Fox, the Sox won 94 games and an American League pennant, but they didn't have enough "Go Go"–or hitting–to get past the Los Angeles Dodgers in a six-game classic.

The most memorable game of the 1959 Series for Chicago fans was the opener, when the White Sox stormed to an 11-0 win behind the pitching of Early Wynn and Gerry Staley and the slugging of first baseman Ted Kluszewski, who homered twice and drove in five runs. Chicago's only other victory came in Game 5 when Bob Shaw, Billy Pierce and Dick Donovan combined to shut out Sandy Koufax and the Dodgers, 1-0.

After winning Game 1 in 1959, things went downhill for the Sox. Left fielder Al Smith's Game 2 beer bath (above) after a Charlie Neal homer symbolized the frustration of the Dodgers' six-game victory.

Game 1 of the 1959 World Series, an 11-0 Chicago romp over the Dodgers, featured a pair of home runs by Sox strongman Ted Kluszewski.

PAST CHAMPIONS 11

THE REGULAR

Several of the 39 players who entered spring training on Chicago's 40-man roster never played a major league game in 2005. Others became key figures in the team's unexpected run to a World Series championship.

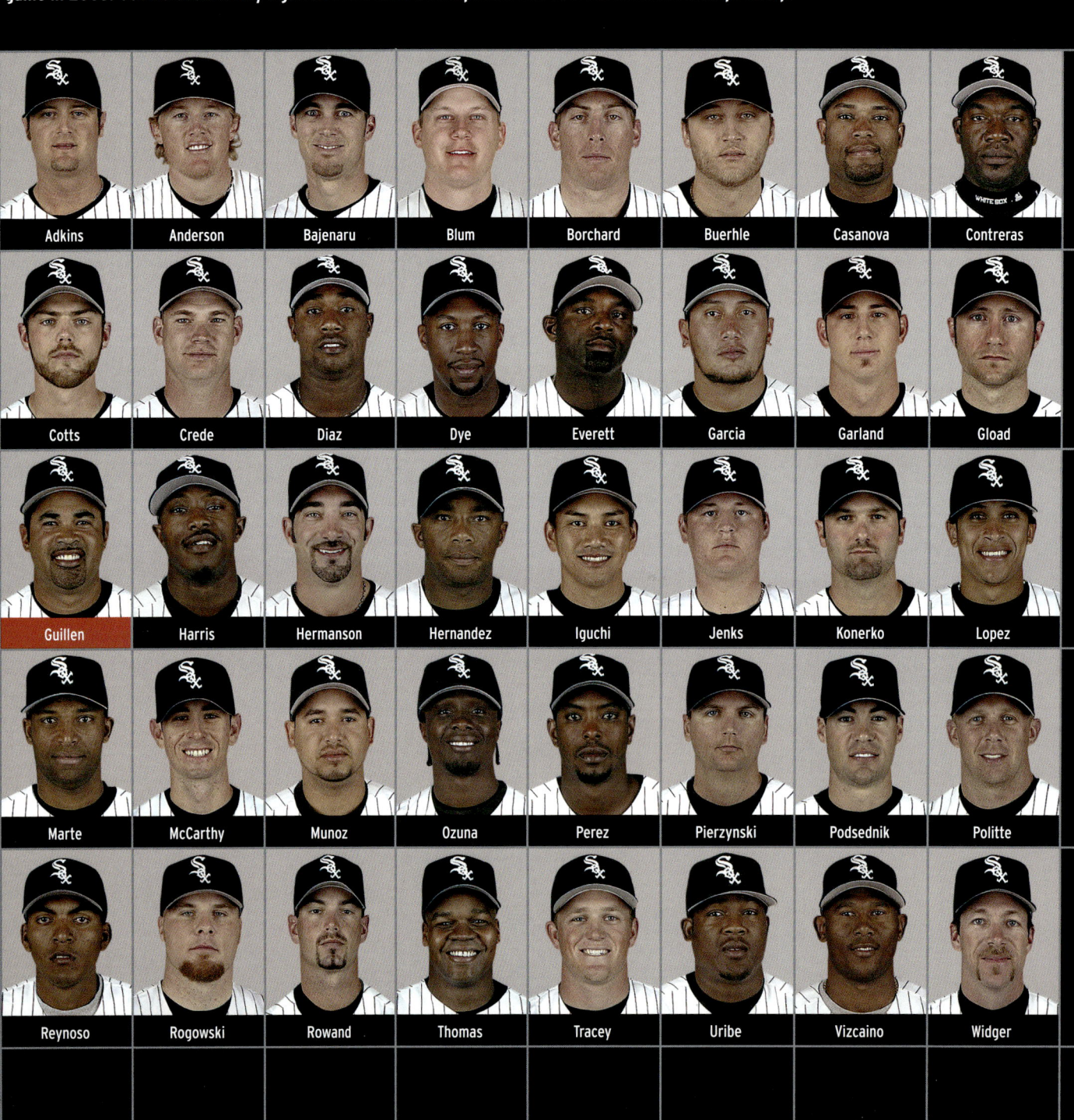

Adkins	Anderson	Bajenaru	Blum	Borchard	Buerhle	Casanova	Contreras	
Cotts	Crede	Diaz	Dye	Everett	Garcia	Garland	Gload	
Guillen	Harris	Hermanson	Hernandez	Iguchi	Jenks	Konerko	Lopez	
Marte	McCarthy	Munoz	Ozuna	Perez	Pierzynski	Podsednik	Politte	
Reynoso	Rogowski	Rowand	Thomas	Tracey	Uribe	Vizcaino	Widger	

12 THE PRIDE OF CHICAGO

SEASON

REGULAR SEASON 13

2005 REGULAR SEASON

THE PLAN: Sox

Ozzie Guillen made a breakthrough discovery during his first season as a major league manager: He had a problem sitting back and waiting for his players to hit the long ball.

Some nights in 2004, the White Sox would light up the sky with fireworks, hitting home run after home run. Fans loved the team's explosiveness, but Guillen always was wary. Other nights–too many, by Guillen's estimate–there weren't enough homers. He would sit on his hands and wait; with a one-dimensional offense, he had no choice.

If there is one weak spot in Guillen's game, it's patience. So toward the end of another second-place season on Chicago's South Side, Guillen pleaded with general manager Ken Williams to give him a 2005 team that would allow him to manage. He wanted to hit and run, bunt, steal bases. He wanted to create action instead of wait for it.

This change in team personality would require more than tinkering on Williams' part. A major overhaul was in order. Guillen would need a legitimate leadoff hitter, a versatile No. 2 hitter and a roster full of players with team-first egos.

"What we had been doing wasn't working," Williams said of a company plan built around power. Williams remembered the power blackout that engulfed the White

THE PRIDE OF CHICAGO

change course

THE CELL Chicago fans in search of a good time and winning baseball in 2005 discovered U.S. Cellular Field was the place to be.

REGULAR SEASON 15

2005 REGULAR SEASON

KEN WILLIAMS AND OZZIE GUILLEN

The 2005 White Sox were the product of a Williams (above) makeover that reduced the reliance on power and allowed Guillen (right) to create offense with a more aggressive small-ball style.

Sox during their most recent trip to the postseason. A turbo-charged lineup that led the majors in runs during the 2000 season had no backup plan when the home runs didn't come during a three-game sweep by the Seattle Mariners in the American League Division Series.

The Sox should have moved to a more balanced attack that next season, but the hitters' ballpark they call home made it tough to let go of the home run approach. Guillen finally broke up the marriage.

THE PRIDE OF CHICAGO

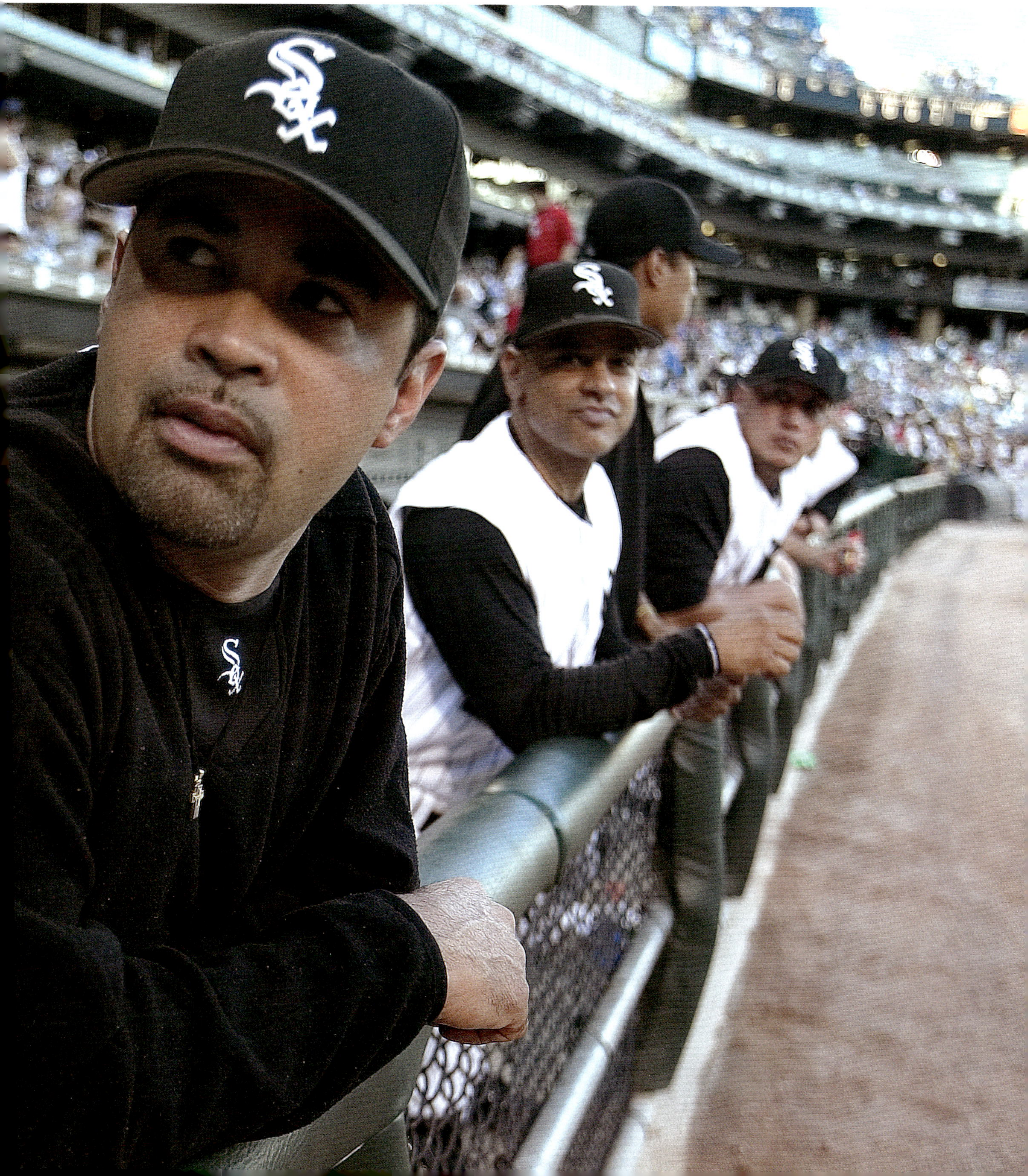

2005 REGULAR SEASON

'This year, forget all that rah-rah stuff,' said Guillen. 'We are focused on winning the division from the first day.'

"We hit a lot of home runs, but so what?" Guillen asked. "We had no leadoff hitter, no speed, we had a lot of holes to fill."

Williams focused on building his team around strong pitching. He began that process during the 2004 season when he acquired righthander Freddy Garcia from the Mariners (in June) and righthander Jose Contreras from the New York Yankees (in July). In December, October-tested veteran Orlando Hernandez was signed as a free agent. Not only did El Duque complete the rotation, he showed that Williams had an eye planted firmly on October.

Williams now had five legitimate starters: Mark Buehrle, Garcia, Hernandez, Contreras and Jon Garland. But the bullpen also was a concern. Shingo Takatsu had replaced the erratic Billy Koch as closer in 2004 and his numbers were solid: 19 saves in 20 chances. But organization insiders believed that Takatsu's gimmicky changeup would have a short shelf life in the majors. The Sox needed a safety net and found it with the early December free-agent signing of former San Francisco Giants closer Dustin Hermanson.

Less than a week later, Williams pulled off a trade that sent shock waves through Chicago. Power-hitting left fielder Carlos Lee was dealt to the Milwaukee Brewers for leadoff hitter Scott Podsednik and righthanded reliever Luis Vizcaino. Right fielder Magglio Ordonez already had taken his big bat into free agency. Designated hitter Frank Thomas, still nursing a surgically repaired ankle, wasn't expected back until June. How could the Sox lose Ordonez, Thomas and Lee and expect to contend?

Williams got roasted by the Chicago media. According to critics, a team that had

THE PRIDE OF CHICAGO

THE ACQUISITIONS

When Ken Williams introduced new second baseman Tadahito Iguchi (below), he filled the need for a solid No. 2 hitter. Other key newcomers included (right, top to bottom) catcher A.J. Pierzynski, reliever Luis Vizcaino, closer Dustin Hermanson, speedy leadoff man Scott Podsednik and starting pitcher Orlando 'El Duque' Hernandez.

REGULAR SEASON 19

2005 REGULAR SEASON

The first

been a contender for five years now looked like a fourth-place club with a hybrid engine. Williams offered no apologies. Lee was going to earn $8 million in 2005, or $6 million more than Podsednik and Vizcaino combined. The trade freed up money to fill other needs. Guillen's team now had a pesky leadoff hitter in Podsednik, but this shift to a small-ball strategy needed one more ingredient. After cutting off negotiations with Japanese second baseman Tadahito Iguchi, Williams dialed long distance to acquire the versatile No. 2 hitter that he thought would complete his offensive makeover.

One other key consideration needed to be addressed. During the up-and-down 2004 season, the Sox listened to criticism that they lacked the heart to match the fiery Minnesota Twins. Williams needed to inject a spirited personality in his clubhouse. So controversial catcher A.J. Pierzynski—a villain in Chicago during his days with the Twins and labeled a clubhouse cancer during his 2004 season with the San Francisco Giants—was signed as a free agent. The Sox got an offensive-minded catcher and a take-no-prisoners attitude for their laid-back clubhouse.

Williams, of course, was ripped again for sprinkling a bad seed in his garden. But Guillen just sat back and admired the new landscaping. This was the team he craved. Before spring training, Guillen tried to quiet critics with some slap-in-the-face reality.

"Last year, I was blind," he said. "Everything sounded great, but I didn't have an opportunity to see what I actually had. For me, it's easier to go to spring training knowing what you have. Last year, it was, 'Rah, rah, good thing we have Ozzie.' This year, forget all that rah-rah stuff. We are focused on winning the division from the first day."

THE PRIDE OF CHICAGO

Starting with their opening day victory over Cleveland,
the White Sox spent every day of the 2005 season in first place.

half

Buehrle's eight two-hit innings in a 1-0 opening day victory over Cleveland provided the perfect teaser for the next seven months—strong starting pitching and just enough hitting. Starting with that victory, the White Sox spent every day of the 2005 season in first place.

The first major turning point came with a victory over the Twins on April 18. Contreras labored through 4⅔ innings that day, throwing 104 pitches, but two Carl Everett home runs, including a tiebreaking shot in the sixth inning, propelled the Sox to a 5-4 win. They grabbed sole possession of first place in the American League Central and never shared the top spot again.

That victory—in which the Twins stranded 10 runners and the Sox left one—ignited the first of three eight-game winning streaks in the first half. Everything Guillen and Williams promised would emerge from the painful rebuilding was coming true. Podsednik was getting on base, distracting pitchers and providing a steady stream of fastballs for Iguchi, his perfect 2-hole complement. With that pesky 1-2 punch leading the charge through a 17-7 April, the White Sox recorded 10 one-run victories. As center fielder Aaron Rowand boasted, "Our motto is: Never score any more runs than you have to."

The pitching was even better than advertised. Garland went from fifth starter to first-half ace, going 8-0 in his first eight

OPENING DAY

The White Sox kick-started their 2005 season at U.S. Cellular Field with patriotic pageantry and a 1-0 victory over the Indians. They would never fall out of the A.L. Central Division lead.

REGULAR SEASON 21

2005 REGULAR SEASON

starts. Buehrle was 7-1 in his first nine, Hernandez 7-1 after 10 starts and Garcia 9-3 by July 15. Then there was Contreras. He didn't get a decision until his sixth start–a May 5 victory over Kansas City–but had a 2.60 ERA over that span.

The notion of small ball was replaced by smart ball–or Ozzie Ball. The Sox were going to steal bases, hit and run and squeeze the most out of every at-bat and runner. Opponents were left scratching their heads. This team was much easier to play against when all you had to worry about was keeping the ball in the park. Now, a runner on first base–especially if it was Podsednik–turned into a major headache.

The White Sox, in reality, never truly abandoned the home run. Station-to-station baseball does have its limits. But there's a lot to be said for picking your spots and exhibiting good timing–both of which the Sox managed to do well in 2005. Take, for example, their 5-3 victory over the Los Angeles Dodgers on June 18. Pierzynski, after almost fouling out to end the game in defeat, delivered a two-out, full-count, two-run homer off Yhency Brazoban in what he called his first "walk-off anything." Every game, it seemed, a new star emerged, whether it was shortstop Juan Uribe, third baseman Joe Crede or right fielder Jermaine Dye.

"A big key to our success all season is (that) somebody new stepped up and made big plays," said Podsednik. "That has been one of our strengths."

Yet every step of the way, the national media just kept waiting for the downsized Sox to crumble. By mid-May, it was clear this team was headed to the playoffs. The starting pitching was too good, the bullpen too solid, the offense too balanced to allow the Sox to suffer an extended losing streak. If this Sox team could stay healthy, Guillen's dream of a Central Division title appeared to be a lock.

FIRST-HALF STARS

The new-look offense was ignited by Scott Podsednik (22), who often made opponents look foolish with his speed and aggressiveness. But the first-half surprise was No. 5 starter Jon Garland, who won his first eight decisions and reached the All-Star break with a 13-4 record.

Through a 17-7 April, the White Sox recorded 10 one-run victories. As center fielder Aaron Rowand boasted, 'Never score any more runs than you have to.'

22 THE PRIDE OF CHICAGO

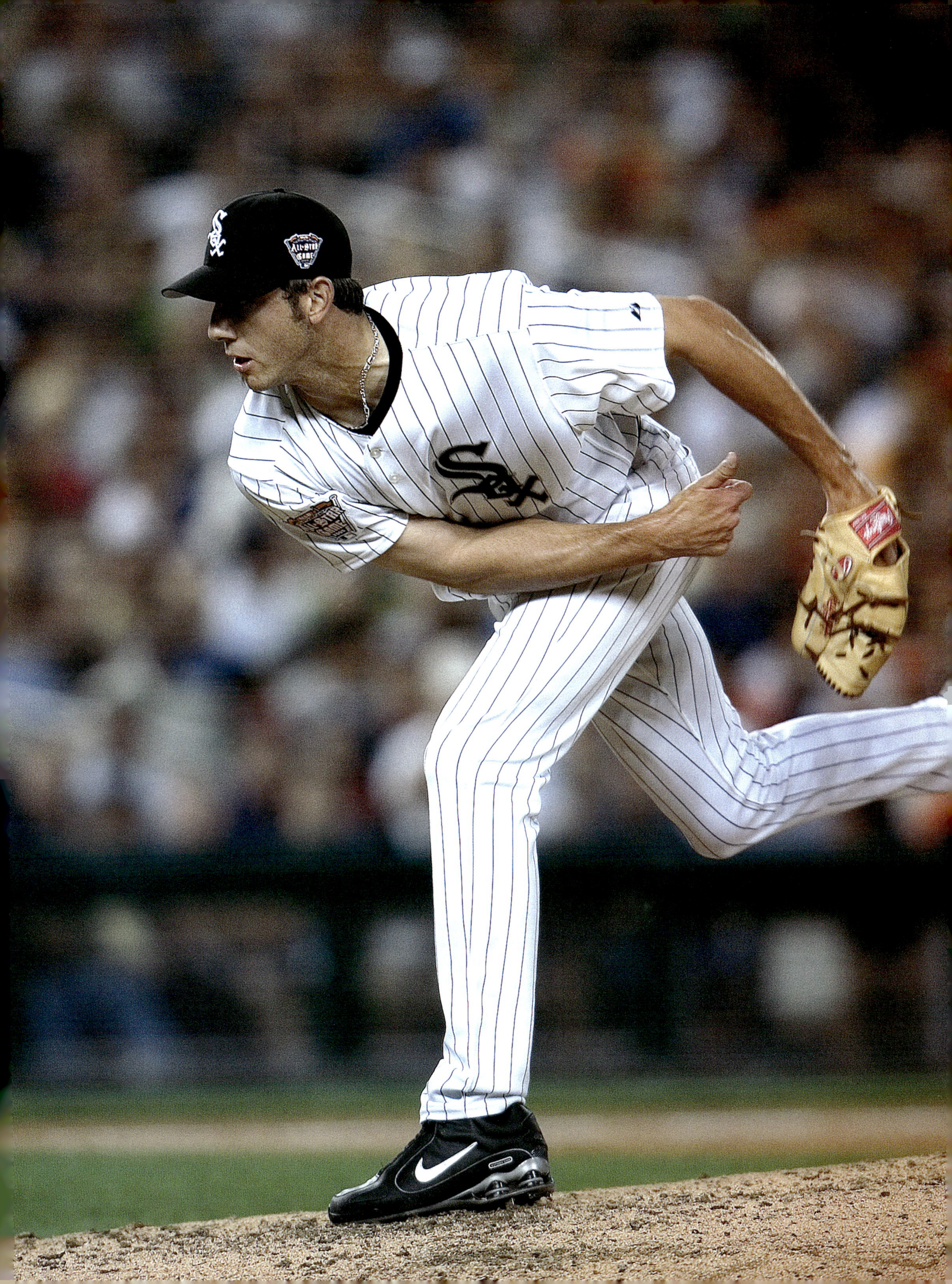

2005 REGULAR SEASON

The All-Stars

If Guillen had his way, the Sox would not have sent any players to the All-Star Game in Detroit. He liked the idea of not having a star player singled out. And with a big-picture goal of the postseason looming large, he preferred that his players take a three-day rest.

No such luck. Buehrle, Garland, Podsednik and Paul Konerko all were chosen to represent the American League. Buehrle was the A.L.'s starting pitcher and earned the victory. All four players were deserving, but Garland and Podsednik were the brightest stars of the first half.

Garland took a 13-4 record and 3.38 ERA into the All-Star Game. He was the first White Sox pitcher to win his first eight starts since John Whitehead in 1935. Along the way, critics stopped calling him mediocre. His laid-back personality no longer was seen as a liability. When he arrived in Detroit for the All-Star Game, Garland immediately cut off questions about his California-cool demeanor.

"You think I don't care out there?" Garland said. "Play against me, you'll find out."

Podsednik stole 59 bases in his first Chicago season—11 fewer than his career high in 2004—but his presence was definitely felt. When he stole a base, the Sox were 27-11. When he stole two or more, they were 9-4. And when he scored a run, they were 42-16. He never hit a home run in the regular season, which seemed to be a perfect ingredient to his small-ball recipe.

"There are not too many guys like him who are just flat-out game-changers," Rowand said.

Mark Buehrle (right), the A.L. starter and winner in the All-Star Game, was joined on the squad by Jon Garland, Paul Konerko and Scott Podsednik. Ozzie Guillen (above) would have preferred his players to stay home and rest.

THE PRIDE OF CHICAGO

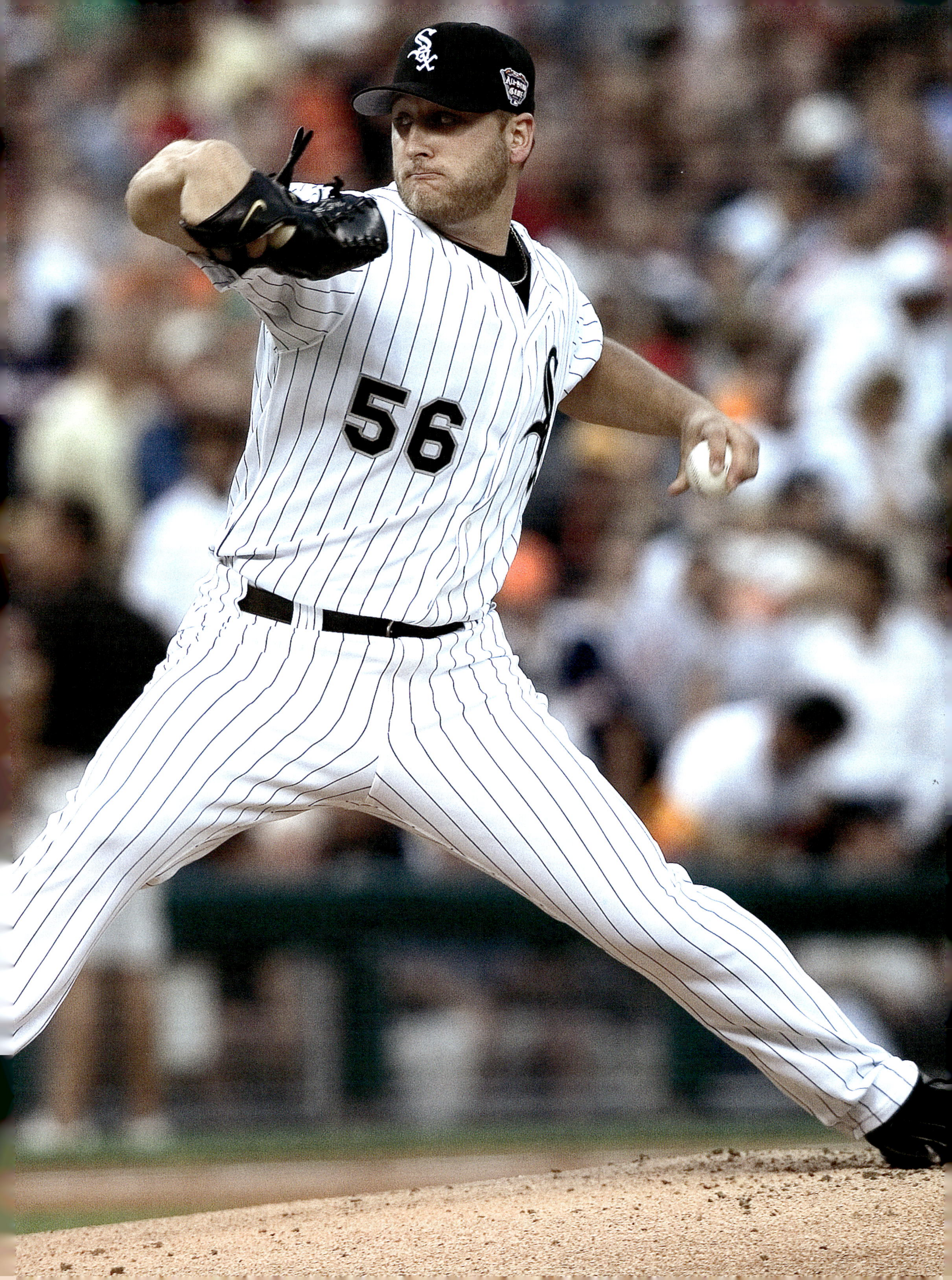
56

2005 REGULAR SEASON

26   THE PRIDE OF CHICAGO

Big Hurt's return

The Sox got off to their big start without their biggest star. Frank Thomas opened the season on the disabled list, recovering from offseason surgery on his left ankle. Everett assumed the designated hitter duties and did a solid job in the first half. For the first time since he arrived in 1990, the White Sox proved they could thrive without Thomas, the face of the club and Chicago's only remaining baseball icon after Sammy Sosa's departure from the Cubs.

After an 11-game stint at Class AAA Charlotte, Thomas proclaimed himself ready. He was activated from the disabled list May 30—the same day the team picked up Guillen's contract option for 2006 and added two more seasons and an option year that could extend it through 2009. Thomas was welcomed by a sellout crowd of 38,685 at U.S. Cellular Field with a rousing standing ovation as he walked to the plate for his first at-bat of 2005. Thomas was clearly moved.

"It brought a tear to my eye," he said. "The fans showed how much they care."

Unfortunately, Thomas' season ended on July 21 when he suffered a second fracture of his ankle. In 34 games, he hit only .219 but contributed 12 home runs and 26 RBIs. "It's real painful ... in the gut," Thomas said of his shortened season. "The biggest question I was asked all year was, 'Are these guys for real?' I knew when I came back in that they were for real. That's why I was so happy to get back."

FRANK THOMAS

Injured most of the season, the Sox's highest profile player contributed 12 homers in 34 games before breaking his ankle.

REGULAR SEASON 27

2005 REGULAR SEASON

The second half

Flexing their muscle after the All-Star break, the White Sox opened the second half with four wins over the Indians—their first four-game sweep in Cleveland since 1963. At this point, the second half seemed just a matter of crossing days off the calendar before throwing a clinching party in early or mid-September.

By August 1, the Sox had stretched their lead in the Central to a season-high 15 games. The Twins had lost superstar Torii Hunter for the season. The Indians looked awful. The Tigers were about to self-destruct. The Royals were the worst team in baseball.

What could go wrong for a White Sox team that hadn't suffered a losing streak longer than three games in the first four months?

Trouble began on August 12, when the White Sox blew a 4-0 lead at Fenway Park. Two home runs by David Ortiz helped the Red Sox rally and hold on for a 9-8 victory that started a season-high seven-game losing streak. By September 15—after a 7-5 loss to the Royals—their lead over the hard-charging Indians had dropped to $4\frac{1}{2}$ games and Guillen was livid. His team had lost six of seven, including two straight to the lowly Royals. It wasn't just the losing, but how the Sox were doing it.

In the September 15 loss, Buehrle labored through $6\frac{1}{3}$ innings, allowing four runs, nine hits and two walks. His second-half record dropped to 5-5. Pierzynski and Everett were thrown out after making baserunning blunders. Guillen was furious.

"We're playing lousy baseball on the bases, pitching, everything," Guillen said after the game. "There's no doubt about it. We really flat-out stink. It's not the same team I've been watching all year."

The second-half slide stirred up talk in Chicago that the White Sox were headed for the biggest collapse in baseball history.

The second-half slide stirred up talk in Chicago that the White Sox were headed for the biggest collapse in baseball history. The term "choke" was getting tossed around and players bristled. But with the Indians coming to town for a September 19-21 showdown series, the lead had dropped to $3\frac{1}{2}$ games. The Sox lost the first game, 7-5, and fans started discussing the wild-card possibilities. But Crede belted a leadoff home run in the 10th inning of the second game for a 7-6 victory that assured the Indians would leave town no closer than $2\frac{1}{2}$ games.

The Indians won the series finale. And an 11-inning loss to the Twins the next night dropped the Sox's lead to $1\frac{1}{2}$ games—their smallest since before they beat Detroit on May 1. Then, when the Sox needed it most, Contreras stepped forward, continuing his second-half mastery. Facing the Twins on September 23, the talented righthander pitched the best game of his major league career. He allowed six hits in his first career complete game and solidified his standing as the new staff ace.

The victory started a stretch of eight wins in the final 10 regular-season games to close out the season. The White Sox clinched the division title with a 4-2 victory over the Tigers on September 29. The Sox held a muted celebration on the field—insisting they were saving their biggest celebration for the World Series.

But there was huge relief that the second-half slump was ended in time for a clinching party before a three-game, regular season-closing series in Cleveland. "I thought it would come down to the last week," Konerko said. "I didn't think we were going to blow a 15-game lead or have Cleveland take it away from us, however you want to look at it. But I thought this division would come down to the last week. Whether it was us and Cleveland, Cleveland and Minnesota, us and Minnesota, maybe Detroit sneaking in there."

THE PRIDE OF CHICAGO

Contreras developed into one of the magical stories during a magical season. At the All-Star break, Contreras had a 4-5 record and a 4.26 ERA. He was the weakest link on a strong pitching staff. One of Williams' midseason goals was to pull off a trade that would add a reliever or veteran bat to his lineup. He was willing—even eager—to package Contreras as the bait for any deal.

It's a good thing he couldn't find takers. Contreras won each of his last eight regular-season starts and was the only consistent starter during the slide that began in August. By the end of September, it was clear he was Chicago's ace entering the postseason after going 11-2 with a 2.96 ERA in 15 second-half starts.

"He's not the same pitcher he was with the Yankees. I guarantee that," Red Sox slugger David Ortiz said after Contreras pitched the White Sox to a 14-2 rout in Game 1 of the American League Division Series. "He's not just throwing the ball. He's spotting the ball, using all of his stuff."

The Contreras revival

JOSE CONTRERAS

The second-half Jose Contreras was much different than the first: He was 11-2 over his last 15 starts. "He's not the same pitcher he was with the Yankees," slugger David Ortiz said after his Red Sox got shut down by the righthander in Game 1 of the A.L. Division Series.

REGULAR SEASON

2005 REGULAR SEASON

Upside to slide

Though no one was willing to admit it at the time, the second-half slide was the best thing that could have happened to a White Sox team that faced little adversity for most of the season. Instead of cruising into the playoffs on autopilot, the Sox learned how to fight when facing adversity. They began doing the little things—a walk or even a fielder's choice—that often turned into decisive innings in their outstanding first half.

It helped that Podsednik, who was battling a groin injury during much of the slide, returned to his pesky ways. Though some fans and plenty of media were ready to give up on the Sox, they never lost their confidence—or poise.

"Through all of the good times and the tough times, this group stuck together," Rowand said. "Through all of the choke this and everything else that was said, it was easy to go ahead and say we had great team chemistry at the beginning of the season when we were winning ballgames. But this team really stuck together when the chips were down and we weren't playing as well together as we knew we could."

Along the way, the Sox discovered a new closer in rookie righthander Bobby Jenks. With Hermanson's lower back a major concern, the Sox needed a new ninth-inning man. In his first season as a reliever, the 24-year-old Jenks showed he could handle the pressure.

The last order of business was deciding who would get the final postseason roster spot—rookie righthander Brandon McCarthy or the October-tested Hernandez. McCarthy had been a solid starter down the stretch,

Instead of cruising into the playoffs on autopilot, the Sox learned how to fight when facing adversity.

LATE MOVES

The White Sox's late-season skid forced manager Ozzie Guillen to make several decisions that would help his team in the playoffs. Young righthander Bobby Jenks (above) took over the closer role from Dustin Hermanson, and postseason-savvy Orlando Hernandez (26) was awarded a roster spot over impressive rookie Brandon McCarthy (far right).

THE PRIDE OF CHICAGO

but Hernandez already had compiled a 9-3 record and 2.65 ERA in the postseason. Plus he pitched well in two relief appearances in the last week of the regular season. The coaching staff fought hard for Hernandez to get the final spot and Williams finally agreed. It turned out to be a pivotal decision.

Once the White Sox had eased into the playoffs they relaxed and handled a first-round sweep of the Red Sox with the looseness that had carried them through the first half. The feeling returned that there was no stopping this wire-to-wire champion.

"The best thing that could have happened to this team is what happened the last three weeks (of the regular season)," Konerko said. "After what happened the last three, four weeks of the season, it's like we have a second life."

REGULAR SEASON 31

2005 REGULAR SEASON

JOE CREDE ▶

Forget that .252 average. Third baseman Crede hit 22 home runs from his spot in the lower third of the batting order and was always dangerous in the clutch.

NEAL COTTS ▼

The lefthanded Cotts appeared in a team-high 69 games and posted a 1.94 ERA as Ozzie Guillen's primary situational guy.

32   THE PRIDE OF CHICAGO

CLIFF POLITTE ▼

The hard-throwing righthander, a former big-league closer, was used in a variety of relief roles in 2005, appearing in 68 games and carving out a 7-1 record with a 2.00 ERA.

◀ JERMAINE DYE

The strong-armed right fielder was not too shabby with the bat in 2005, either. Dye hit 31 home runs and batted .274.

REGULAR SEASON   33

2005 REGULAR SEASON

DUSTIN HERMANSON ▼

Hermanson, a key offseason pickup, held the closer job through much of the season before suffering back problems and giving way to Bobby Jenks. Hermanson recorded 15 straight saves before blowing his first and finished with 34.

CARL EVERETT ▶

Sometimes unpredictable and volatile, the designated hitter/outfielder supplied a lefthanded power threat to the White Sox lineup. Everett's 23 homers ranked third on the team.

FREDDY GARCIA ▲

Garcia, a 2004 pickup from Seattle, fashioned a steady 14-8 record and was a key member of the White Sox's rebuilt 2005 rotation.

2005 REGULAR SEASON

▼ DAMASO MARTE
The former lights-out bullpen lefthander struggled with his command and saw his stock drop in 2005. But Marte still appeared in 66 games and was effective in situational roles.

TIMO PEREZ ▲
While Perez didn't hit much in his second season with the White Sox, he provided depth in the outfield and late-game speed.

◄ WILLIE HARRIS
The versatile and speedy infielder batted .256 in 56 games off the bench.

THE PRIDE OF CHICAGO

▼ TADAHITO IGUCHI

The talented second baseman, signed out of Japan in the offseason, provided stability in both the field and lineup. The man Ozzie Guillen declared his team MVP did all the fundamental things managers appreciate: bunt, move runners, hit and run—and his 15 home runs were a nice bonus.

2005 REGULAR SEASON

PAUL ▶ KONERKO

Whether running the bases (14), playing first base or swinging the bat, Konerko emerged in 2005 as the White Sox team leader. His statistics confirm that role: .283, 40 homers and 100 RBIs.

38   THE PRIDE OF CHICAGO

◄ PABLO OZUNA

Versatility and speed were the primary contributions of Ozuna, who played every infield position and in the outfield while often entering games late as a pinch runner.

A.J. PIERZYNSKI ►

Brought in to inject fire in a laid-back clubhouse, Pierzynski met expectations and delivered 18 home runs.

2005 REGULAR SEASON

SHINGO TAKATSU

Hitters caught up to Takatsu, who had saved 19 games in 20 chances in 2004. With the arrival of Dustin Hermanson and emergence of Bobby Jenks, the Japanese sidearmer was released in August.

LUIS VIZCAINO ▼

The workhorse righthander, who was picked up from Milwaukee in the Carlos Lee-Scott Podsednik deal, made 65 appearances with a 3.73 ERA.

AARON ROWAND ▲

The Sox's much-improved middle defense was anchored by the steady center fielder, who also drove in 69 runs.

40   THE PRIDE OF CHICAGO

JUAN URIBE ▶

The athletic and quick Uribe (5) anchored the Sox's middle defense from his shortstop position, and his dangerous bat contributed 16 homers and 71 RBIs.

THE DIVISION SERIES

42 THE PRIDE OF CHICAGO

DIVISION SERIES 43

GAME 1

A.L. DIVISION SERIES

WHITE SOX 14, RED SOX 2

```
BOSTON    000 200 000    2  9  0    L: CLEMENT (0-1, 21.60)
CHICAGO   501 204 02x   14 11  1    W: CONTRERAS (1-0, 2.35)
```

White Sox steal Boston's thunder in opening romp

Enough small-ball talk. The Red Sox watched Chicago hitters explode for five homers—two by A.J. Pierzynski (12, right) and one apiece by Juan Uribe (5), Scott Podsednik (22) and Paul Konerko (14)—in a 14-2 romp in the Division Series opener.

On the front of this A.J. Pierzynski T-shirt are the words: "Ozzie Ball Means" ... And on the back: "Heart, Brains, Balls."

So that's it. Forget all that small-ball talk. Ozzie Ball, essentially, is doing what it takes to win.

That sometimes does mean running. In the regular season, the Sox got 59 stolen bases and daily thrills from leadoff hitter Scott Podsednik. Every time the speedy left fielder reaches base at U.S. Cellular Field, the excitement builds among White Sox fans who anticipate that something is about to happen.

But Ozzie Ball also means home runs. The White Sox

THE PRIDE OF CHICAGO

October 4, U.S. Cellular Field

A.L. DIVISION SERIES, GAME 1   45

GAME 1
2005 A.L. DIVISION SERIES

PIERZYNSKI: 3-for-3, 2 HR, 4 RBIs

hit 200 during the regular season, the fourth highest total in the American League and one more than the Red Sox.

In the opening game of the A.L. Division Series, the White Sox went the long-ball route. They hit five home runs—an A.L. club Division Series record—and hammered the Red Sox, 14-2. Pierzynski led the way with two while Paul Konerko, Juan Uribe and Podsednik hit one apiece. Posednik's was his first of the season.

The victory was the White Sox's first in a postseason home game since the 1959 World Series.

The White Sox wasted no time starting the party against Red Sox starter Matt Clement. Podsednik was hit by a pitch, moved to second on a sacrifice, stole third and scored on a grounder by Konerko. Another hit batsman and singles by Carl Everett and Aaron Rowand scored a second run, and Pierzynski followed with a three-run, opposite-field blast. The rout was on.

Clement did not make it through the fourth inning and left with the White Sox leading, 8-2. The Sox added four runs in the sixth and two in the eighth to set a club record for runs in a postseason game.

White Sox starter Jose Contreras continued his late-season brilliance by limiting the Red Sox to two runs before leaving with two out in the eighth. Effectively using his slider and splitter to complement his 95-mph fastball, Contreras gave up eight hits, struck out six and didn't walk anyone.

It was a pretty good showing for the pitcher who was practically run out of New York last season because of his struggles against the Red Sox. And an even better one for a team that had gone 12 years since its last postseason victory.

Game 1 was ugly for Red Sox starter Matt Clement, who departed in the fourth inning (left) with an 8-2 deficit. The White Sox cruised behind the pitching of former Yankee Jose Contreras (52), who slowed down David Ortiz and Boston's other big hitters.

Iguchi's surprise was a bad one for the Red Sox

The Red Sox were rallying, having cut a 6-0 lead to 6-2 in the fourth inning, and they had Kevin Millar on second with nobody out.

Bill Mueller knew it was his job to move Millar to third. And he did exactly what he was supposed to do—he hit a grounder to second. But White Sox second baseman Tadahito Iguchi had other ideas. Instead of going to first base for the sure out, Iguchi threw to third and nailed Millar for the first out of the inning. Just like that, Boston's momentum was killed. No other Red Sox player reached second in the inning and only two got that far the rest of the game.

In the White Sox dugout, manager Ozzie Guillen was seen shaking his head in disapproval over Iguchi's decision—until the play was completed. Guillen said he went from "No, no, no to that a boy, good. I don't think it was the right play but it worked out pretty good for us."

Millar said it was the first time he could remember that play being made all season. "It was risky but it turned out to be a good play," Millar said. "After that out, that beat us pretty good."

White Sox third baseman Joe Crede looks for an out call after tagging Kevin Millar on a surprising throw from second baseman Tadahito Iguchi.

THE PRIDE OF CHICAGO

GAME **1** 2005 A.L. DIVISION SERIES

A.L. DIVISION SERIES, GAME 1   47

GAME 2

A.L. DIVISION SERIES

WHITE SOX 5, RED SOX 4

```
BOSTON    202 000 000   4 9 1   L: WELLS (0-1, 2.70)
CHICAGO   000 050 00x   5 9 0   W: BUEHRLE (1-0, 5.14)
```

Iguchi, Jenks step up as White Sox win again

Tadahito Iguchi's three-run homer in the fifth inning supplied the tying and winning runs but the real hero in this 5-4 White Sox victory was rookie closer Bobby Jenks.

In his first postseason appearance—the 24-year-old started the 2005 season in the minors and didn't start closing until September—Jenks shut down the game's most potent offense in the eighth and ninth innings. The first batter he faced was Manny Ramirez, who lined to center. Jenks allowed only one baserunner in each inning to earn the save and put the White Sox in command of the Division Series.

Jenks said he was more nervous in the sixth and seventh innings than when he took the mound. "I had that bad feeling in my stomach, like you need to burp," he said. And the jog in from the bullpen, as the fans chanted, "Bobby ... Bobby?"

"Just like any other," he said, quickly adding with a smile, "Not really, but that's what I tried to play in my mind."

"I've got to throw my best bullpen guy against the best hitter they have," said manager Ozzie Guillen, who continued to make the right moves. When Jenks is throwing strikes, which has been his problem, he can dominate any hitter. His fastball has been clocked at 103 mph and he has a plus-curveball. The pitch hitters

Bobby Jenks' first postseason appearance was both animated and successful. The young closer showed his saving grace by shutting down the potent Red Sox for two innings in Game 2.

THE PRIDE OF CHICAGO

October 5, U.S. Cellular Field

GAME 2: 2005 A.L. DIVISION SERIES

IGUCHI: 2-for-4, HR, 3 RBIs

Center fielder Johnny Damon (above) had two hits and scored twice as the Red Sox jumped to an early 4-0 lead, but a three-run, fifth-inning homer by Tadahito Iguchi (15, right) gave Chicago a 5-4 lead and Boston lefty David Wells a headache.

fear most, however, is his cutter.

White Sox starter Mark Buehrle gave up two runs in the first inning and two more in the third before holding the Red Sox scoreless for four. The White Sox, trailing 4-0, rallied in the fifth when they scored all of their runs on four hits.

They got a big break when former White Sox second baseman Tony Graffanino let a double-play grounder roll through his legs.

Instead of being done for the inning, the White Sox had two runners on and only one out. After Scott Podsednik fouled out, Iguchi hit a 1-1 offering from Red Sox starter David Wells into the seats in left.

Those three runs were the last for either team.

The rest of the game belonged to the hard-throwing closer with the baby face and, on this night, beaming smile.

When Tony Graffanino's fifth-inning error (left) opened the door, Joe Crede and the opportunistic White Sox ran through it.

50 THE PRIDE OF CHICAGO

White Sox 'MVP' could have worn Red Sox

When **Tadahito Iguchi** decided he wanted to leave Japan for the major leagues, the first team he tried out for was the Red Sox. The tryout didn't go well and the contract negotiations went even worse.

A couple of months later, after Iguchi had dropped his asking price and the Red Sox had made other plans, he signed with the White Sox. He struggled early on—one scout wasn't sure Iguchi would make it in the majors—but proved to be an important catalyst for the White Sox after moving into the No. 2 spot in the lineup. Iguchi hit 15 homers and stole 15 bases and, just as important, always was eager to move runners or take pitches so leadoff hitter Scott Podsednik could steal a base.

By season's end, Ozzie Guillen was telling anyone who would listen that Iguchi was his team's most valuable player. "He made the plays, hit the home runs. This kid did everything for the team, and that's what I keep saying," Guillen said.

Guillen was looking pretty smart—again—after Game 2. His MVP hit a curveball from David Wells for a two-out, three-run homer in the fifth inning that proved to be the difference. You can be sure no one in Chicago was unhappy that tryout with the Red Sox last December did not work out too well.

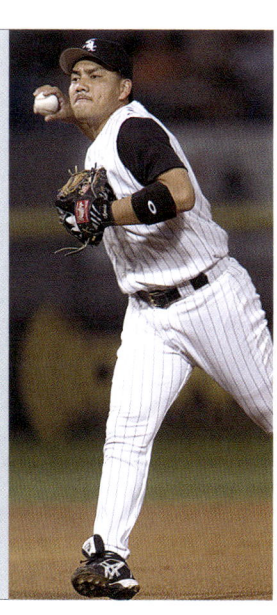

A.L. DIVISION SERIES, GAME 2

GAME 3 — A.L. DIVISION SERIES
WHITE SOX 5, RED SOX 3

```
CHICAGO   002 002 001   5 8 0    W: GARCIA (1-0, 5.40)
BOSTON    000 201 000   3 7 1    L: WAKEFIELD (0-1, 6.75)
```

The White Sox finished off Boston with the magic of Orlando Hernandez, who came out of the bullpen to diffuse a bases-loaded threat and protect a one-run lead. El Duque ended the sixth inning by striking out Johnny Damon (18), who was tagged out by catcher A.J. Pierzynski.

El Duque's rescue is a sweeping success

To win their first postseason series since 1917, the White Sox leaned on a wily veteran. Fenway Park was rocking and the Red Sox were threatening when Orlando "El Duque" Hernandez was summoned from the bullpen. And oh, did Mr. Big Game come through!

Hernandez delivered three scoreless innings to lead the White Sox to a 5-3 victory and a sweep of the defending World Series champions.

"Finally we make another big step," said manager Ozzie Guillen. "I think the people in Chicago should feel proud of these players. They did everything. People are talking about the White Sox again and we should feel good about it."

Just two weeks earlier, the White Sox had seemed on the verge of the biggest collapse in major league

52   THE PRIDE OF CHICAGO

October 7, Fenway Park

GAME 3
2005 A.L. DIVISION SERIES

HERNANDEZ: 3 IP, 1 H, 0 R, 4 SO, 0.00 ERA

54 THE PRIDE OF CHICAGO

history. Their 15-game lead on August 1 had been cut to 1½ games by the Indians, and a season-closing series between the teams loomed big. But Chicago swept that series, and the Division Series showcased the more relaxed White Sox, perhaps a benefit from having survived their late-season scare.

But talk about frightening situations. When Hernandez entered in the sixth inning of Game 3, the White Sox led by one, the Red Sox had the bases loaded and there was—that's right—nobody out.

First up: Jason Varitek. With the count 2-1, he popped up meekly in foul ground between home and first.

Second up: Game 2 goat Tony Graffanino. With the opportunity for redemption, he worked the count full, then fouled off three straight fastballs. Catcher A.J. Pierzynski visited the mound. Hernandez, to Pierzynski's surprise, said he

Orlando Hernandez celebrates his sweeping success with a hug from closer Bobby Jenks (45) and a victory cigar. For manager Ozzie Guillen (above), there was plenty to laugh about.

A.L. DIVISION SERIES, GAME 3   55

GAME 3

2005 A.L. DIVISION SERIES

KONERKO: 1-for-4, HR, 2 RBIs

Boston reliever Mike Timlin shows his frustration (right) after his bad throw allowed A.J. Pierzynski to slide past catcher Jason Varitek with a ninth-inning insurance run. But Paul Konerko's sixth-inning homer (far right) provided the decisive run.

wanted to throw a slider inside. Then he did just that and Graffanino hit a harmless pop in front of second base. Pierzynski pumped his fist as soon as he saw the ball leave Graffanino's bat. El Duque walked in and traded a fist-bump with his catcher.

"Graffanino battled, and I have to resort to my experience. I called for that pitch inside," El Duque said through a translator in the postgame news conference. "My catcher was surprised but I thought that's the only way I could get them out."

Third up: Leadoff hitter Johnny Damon. Another full count. More fouls. Another meeting. This time,

Hernandez's slider dropped inside and to the ground but Damon couldn't check his swing. Strikeout. Inning over. The Sox's 4-3 lead is intact.

El Duque went through the heart of the order in the seventh—striking out Edgar Renteria and David Ortiz before getting Manny Ramirez to ground out— and gave up nothing but a two-out single in the eighth.

The White Sox added an insurance run in the ninth and watched rookie Bobby Jenks pitch a three-up, three-down ninth. The White Sox were on their way to the ALCS for the first time since 1993.

56 THE PRIDE OF CHICAGO

Konerko: The power of one

Fittingly, the home run that made the difference was hit by **Paul Konerko**, the White Sox's leading slugger and stoic leader.

In the top of the sixth, with the score tied, Konerko hit a 1-1 offering from knuckleballer Tim Wakefield over Fenway Park's Green Monster for a two-run homer. The White Sox had a 4-2 lead they would not lose.

"I just tried to stay up tall and let it come into me and swing hard in case I hit it," Konerko said. "That's basically what happened."

Konerko, who spent his early years in Rhode Island, paused at home plate to watch his blast for just an instant. Though he is as humble as major leaguers come, if ever there was a time to admire a home run, this was it.

A.L. DIVISION SERIES, GAME 3 57

THE LEAGUE CHAMPIONSHIP SERIES

A.L. CHAMPIONSHIP SERIES 59

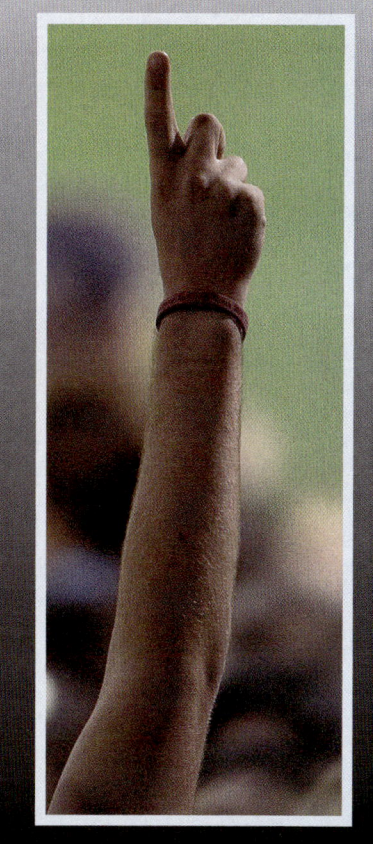

GAME 1

A.L. CHAMPIONSHIP
ANGELS 3, WHITE SOX 2

| LOS ANGELES | 012 000 000 | 3 7 1 | W: BYRD (1-0, 3.00) |
| CHICAGO | 001 100 000 | 2 7 0 | L: CONTRERAS (0-1, 3.24) |

60 THE PRIDE OF CHICAGO

SERIES

October 11, U.S. Cellular Field

Weary Angels sleepwalk past 'flat' Sox in opener

The script favored the well-rested White Sox at U.S. Cellular Field, but Paul Byrd's pitching and a pesky small-ball assault against Jose Contreras (far left) resulted in an unhappy ending.

This certainly wasn't how the White Sox wanted to start the American League Championship Series. Going into Game 1, all the story lines were in their favor:

They were starting their ace, Jose Contreras, winner of nine straight starts.

They were facing an Angels club that had made two cross-country flights in the last two days, and had just learned its 20-game winner, Bartolo Colon, would not pitch in the series.

They would be playing in front of another rockin' sellout at the Cell.

But the Sox didn't give their fans much to cheer about after the game began. They came out flat, made too many mistakes and fell, 3-2, ending their winning streak at eight games dating back to the end of the regular season. Contreras pitched 8⅓ strong innings, allowing three runs on seven hits, but was compromised by a Garret Anderson home run and his own

A.L. CHAMPIONSHIP SERIES, GAME 1   **61**

GAME 1 — 2005 A.L. CHAMPIONSHIP SERIES

CONTRERAS: 8 1/3 IP, 7 H, 3 R, 4 SO

defensive lapse.

The White Sox trailed 1-0 going into the third when the Angels put on a small-ball display of their own. Two singles and a sacrifice put runners on second and third when Orlando Cabrera hit a grounder to third. Joe Crede hesitated just enough to allow Steve Finley to score and Cabrera to reach first. Vladimir Guerrero then hit a grounder to Contreras who, instead of throwing home, fired to second trying to get an inning-ending double play. The Sox forced the hard-sliding Cabrera but were unable to double Guerrero at first as Kennedy scored the Angels' third—and final—run.

"If the ball had been hit a bit slower and I didn't think I had a chance to turn a double play, I would have probably gone home," Contreras told reporters. "But we've turned double plays all season long and can't change anything you've done this season. If we turned that double play we might be talking about something different."

In a game when each team managed only seven hits, several Sox attempts to manufacture runs backfired. In the fifth, Scott Podsednik singled off Angels starter Paul Byrd and was thrown out trying to steal.

A.J. Pierzynski, who had delivered an RBI single earlier in the game, was caught stealing in the seventh when he thought the hit-and-run was on.

The White Sox also put their leadoff man on in each of the last two innings but were unable to get a clutch hit off Angels reliever Scot Shields and closer Francisco Rodriguez.

"We have to come back and play hard," White Sox manager Ozzie Guillen said. "I don't have anything to say about the boys. The boys are playing good, but (the Angels) played better than we did."

Sox manager Ozzie Guillen (left) got a well-deserved ovation when introduced during pregame ceremonies.

62 THE PRIDE OF CHICAGO

The White Sox, so good at manufacturing runs all season, were frustrated in Game 1 by the Angels. Scott Podsednik was tagged out trying to steal (below) in the fifth inning by shortstop Orlando Cabrera, and A.J. Pierzynski was tagged out on a seventh-inning steal attempt (left) by second baseman Adam Kennedy.

GAME 1 — 2005 A.L. CHAMPIONSHIP SERIES

A.L. CHAMPIONSHIP SERIES, GAME 1

GAME 1 — 2005 A.L. CHAMPIONSHIP SERIES

CREDE: 1-for-4, HR, 1 RBI

The Angels were efficient in the opener, doing just enough to win. Orlando Cabrera's infield single (top photo) delivered a third-inning run, and reliever Scot Shields (above) worked two scoreless innings. Closer Francisco Rodriguez pumps his fist (left) after striking out Joe Crede to end the game.

64 THE PRIDE OF CHICAGO

Joe Crede's third-inning homer (below) was one of the Sox's few Game 1 highlights.

Former Sox shortstop Chico Carrasquel, who died in the spring of 2005, was a major influence during Ozzie Guillen's career.

There's crying in baseball

Always upbeat Ozzie Guillen, never one to shy away from a microphone, was silenced and brought to tears by a question at his pregame press conference. Tears of sadness as well as pride.

Well into the press conference, Guillen was asked about his relationship with one of his childhood heroes, Chico Carrasquel, a former White Sox standout who died in the spring of 2005. Carrasquel, the first of several outstanding major league shortstops from Venezuela, became the first Latin player selected to start in an All-Star Game in 1951. Twenty-six years after Carrasquel's retirement, another White Sox shortstop from Venezuela was named A.L. Rookie of the Year. That was Guillen, who would go on to earn three All-Star Game invitations in his 16-year career.

"You're going to make me cry here," Guillen said. "Chico was one of my best friends in Chicago. I think I know where he is right now. He would be proud."

Guillen, head down, then stood up and exited the interview room through a side door.

GAME 1 — 2005 A.L. CHAMPIONSHIP SERIES

A.L. CHAMPIONSHIP SERIES, GAME 1   65

GAME 2

A.L. CHAMPIONSHIP
WHITE SOX 2, ANGELS 1

LOS ANGELES	000 010 000	1 5 3	L: ESCOBAR (0-1, 0.00)
CHICAGO	100 000 001	2 7 1	W: BUEHRLE (1-0, 1.00)

White Sox strike late, thanks to lucky 'bounce'

66 THE PRIDE OF CHICAGO

SERIES

October 12, U.S. Cellular Field

Somewhere along the line, a little luck is needed to play deep into October. In Game 2 of the ALCS, the White Sox got their fair share of good fortune.

The situation: With the score tied at 1 and two out in the ninth inning, A.J. Pierzynski swung at a low pitch from Kelvim Escobar and missed for strike three—or so everyone thought.

Pierzynski took a step toward the White Sox dugout and, realizing umpire Doug Eddings had not called him out, turned and ran to first. Angels catcher Josh Paul, who thought he had caught the ball cleanly (and replays seemed to

The strikeout that wasn't: A.J. Pierzynski swings and misses at Kelvim Escobar's ninth-inning pitch (left) as catcher Josh Paul reaches to catch it. Angels first baseman Darin Erstad (right) asks umpire Doug Eddings why Pierzynski is not out, and manager Mike Scioscia pleads his case (below).

GAME 2
2005 A.L. CHAMPIONSHIP SERIES

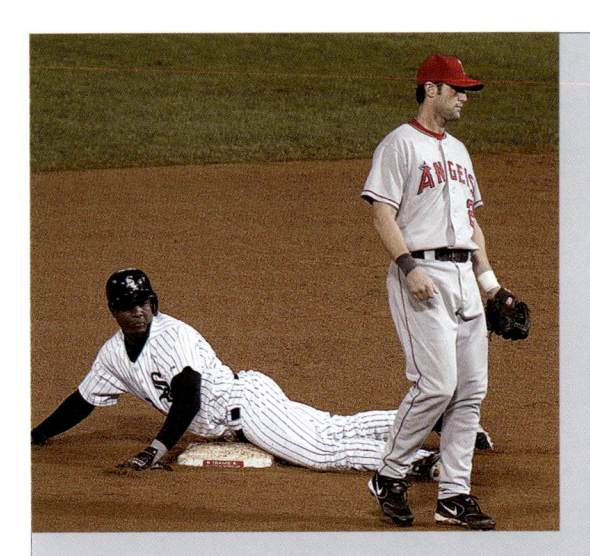

BUEHRLE: 9 IP, 5 H, 1 R, 4 SO

Given new life after A.J. Pierzynski reached first on a ninth-inning strikeout, the Sox scored the winning run when pinch runner Pablo Ozuna stole second base (above) and came home on Joe Crede's two-out double (right), sparking a big celebration.

Crede steps up again

Joe Crede stepped up again. The White Sox third baseman, who delivered his share of big hits in September, came through with the biggest so far in October.

After the storm had cleared from A.J. Pierzynski's strikeout that wasn't, Crede stepped to the plate and made sure there would be no question about the ending

agree), rolled the ball toward the mound as his teammates walked off the field.

The result: After a few minutes of discussion, Pierzynski was ruled safe. Angels manager Mike Scioscia argued his case, to no avail. When action resumed, pinch runner Pablo Ozuna stole second and brought the game to a controversial close when he scored the winning run on Joe Crede's double off the left field wall. The White Sox had their first victory in an ALCS game since 1993 and, more importantly, would not have to dig themselves out of a 2-0 hole with the series shifting to California.

"When the ball bounces your way you have a chance," Sox manager Ozzie Guillen said. "This is a game about inches and we took advantage of the two inches that helped us today. I always say I'd rather be lucky than good."

Pierzynski said he had been victimized by a similar play when he was with the Giants in 2004. "The third strike is in the dirt, you run," he said. "Josh didn't tag me, I think he thought (Eddings) called it, and I just ran, and luckily it worked out."

The White Sox's first run wasn't earned, either. Scott Podsednik led off the game with a comebacker to Angels starter Jarrod Washburn, who threw the ball over his first baseman's head. Podsednik went to second, was sacrificed to third and scored on Jermaine Dye's grounder.

White Sox lefthander Mark Buehrle did not need much help from his offense. He served up a fifth-inning homer to Robb Quinlan but otherwise was masterful for nine innings. He gave up five hits and didn't walk anyone in the first complete game by any pitcher in this postseason.

"Probably one of the best games of my career," said Buehrle, who did not mind being overshadowed by the ninth-inning controversy—as long as it meant a White Sox victory.

THE PRIDE OF CHICAGO

of the tight contest. Reliever Kelvim Escobar had been dominating until Crede lined an 0-2 split-finger fastball off the left field wall to bring in Pablo Ozuna with the winning run. The night before, his fifth-inning homer had put the White Sox on the scoreboard, but he also had made the last out of a 3-2 loss when he struck out facing Angels closer Francisco Rodriguez with a runner on base.

"The biggest part is actually getting the opportunity to be in that situation," Crede said. "(The pitch) hung up in the zone. He had a good splittie, it just didn't drop off the table like he wanted it to."

Tied 1-1 in the ALCS, manager Ozzie Guillen didn't realize the next game at U.S. Cellular Field would be in the World Series.

A.L. CHAMPIONSHIP SERIES, GAME 2 **69**

GAME 2

2005 A.L. CHAMPIONSHIP SERIES

CREDE: 2-for-4, 2 2B, 1 RBI

Pitching and defense dominated in Game 2, which featured a good catch by left fielder Scott Podsednik (left) and a force at second by shortstop Juan Uribe (right) on Jose Molina. The White Sox missed a second-inning opportunity when Aaron Rowand was tagged out at the plate by Molina (top photo) when he tried to score on a ground ball to third base.

THE PRIDE OF CHICAGO

After the smoke had cleared for Mark Buehrle from the pregame celebration (top photo), the Sox scored a first-inning run. Scott Podsednik reached when Angels first baseman Darin Erstad couldn't catch pitcher Jarrod Washburn's errant throw (far left) and eventually scored (above) on a grounder by Jermaine Dye (left).

A.L. CHAMPIONSHIP SERIES, GAME 2

GAME 3 — A.L. CHAMPIONSHIP
WHITE SOX 5, ANGELS 2

CHICAGO	301 010 000	5 11 0	W: GARLAND (1-0, 2.00)
LOS ANGELES	000 002 000	2 4 0	L: LACKEY (0-1, 9.00)

Garland completely baffles Angels

Jon Garland admitted that he was concerned about pitching on 12 days rest. As it turned out, he didn't need to be.

Buoyed by a three-run first inning, Garland took the mound in Game 3 at Angel Stadium and pitched a complete-game, 5-2 victory over Los Angeles. The righthander, working near his childhood home in Granada Hills, ran into trouble only once as he allowed four hits and helped the White Sox take a 2-1 lead in the American League Championship Series.

"Going out there and giving me some quick early runs took the pressure off me a little bit," Garland said. "I was able to go out there and attack the zone."

There was nothing controversial on this night, and there wasn't much suspense after the first inning. Scott Podsednik led off the game with a single on an 0-2 pitch from John Lackey and came home on a one-out double by Jermaine Dye, who extended his postseason hitting streak to five games. Paul Konerko followed Dye with a two-run homer to left-center field and the White Sox were on their way. They added runs in the third on Carl Everett's single to left, and in the fifth on Konerko's single to center. But the night belonged to Garland.

Garland did not allow two baserunners in the same inning until the sixth when, with the Sox up 5-0, he surrendered a two-out, two-run homer to Orlando Cabrera. After the homer, Garland retired the final 10 Angels as the White Sox bullpen enjoyed another night off. The 18-game winner frustrated the Angels by mixing a fastball that topped out at 94 mph with an effective changeup in an 118-pitch outing.

"I trust this kid, and he's coming up to be a pretty good pitcher," White Sox manager Ozzie Guillen said. "I think that's the best I've seen him throw all year long."

Second baseman Tadahito Iguchi helped his cause with strong defense, two hits and two runs scored. In the first, with a runner on, Iguchi was

Front and center in Game 3 was Jon Garland, who allowed only four hits and received well-deserved congratulations from his teammates.

72 THE PRIDE OF CHICAGO

SERIES

October 14, Angel Stadium

A.L. CHAMPIONSHIP SERIES, GAME 3 **73**

GAME 3
2005 A.L. CHAMPIONSHIP SERIES

KONERKO: 3-for-4, HR, 3 RBIs

stationed near the second-base bag when Vladimir Guerrero rapped a grounder that Iguchi turned into an inning-ending double play. In the next inning, Iguchi made a strong relay throw to nail Darin Erstad trying to stretch a double into a triple. Joe Crede made a nice play on a Garret Anderson grounder in the fourth but other than that, Garland was in total control. Like Jose Contreras and Mark Buehrle before him, Garland was successful in large part because he was able to shut down the heart of the Angels' order. After the first three games of the series, Guerrero, Anderson and Bengie Molina had combined for three hits in 33 at-bats.

"That's incredible starting pitching," Angels manager Mike Scioscia said. "It might have been one of the top couple games we've had pitched against us all year. Coming off the heels of what Buehrle did the other night and Contreras in Game 1, those horses they have up front, you know, can pitch."

The first inning was rough for Angels starter John Lackey (top right), who gave up an RBI double to Jermaine Dye (23) and a two-run homer to Paul Konerko (14). Scott Podsednik (above) also got in on the early scoring, as did Carl Everett (8) two innings later.

74 THE PRIDE OF CHICAGO

Sox third baseman Joe Crede awaits the relay from Tadahito Iguchi as Angels runner Darin Erstad goes into his slide. Erstad lost the race with the ball and was tagged out in the second inning while trying to stretch a double into a triple.

A.L. CHAMPIONSHIP SERIES, GAME 3

GAME 3 — 2005 A.L. CHAMPIONSHIP SERIES

GARLAND: 9 IP, 4 H, 2 R, 1 BB, 7 SO

Tadahito Iguchi, who had doubled, races home with a fifth-inning insurance run on a single by Paul Konerko.

THE PRIDE OF CHICAGO

Sox provide a calm after the storm

After their offense had been shut down in the first two games, the White Sox's three-run run first inning in Game 3 provided a turning point—in the game and series—for a number of reasons:

■ In a park where thunder sticks reign and the Ralley Monkey rules, the fast start helped take the crowd out of the game—and really, the rest of the series. The soldout stadium certainly was rocking before Game 3, with fans showing no mercy on umpire Doug Eddings and White Sox catcher A.J. Pierzynski for their roles in the controversial call that helped decide Game 2. A security guard was stationed near Eddings, who was working the right field line. Pierzynski, meanwhile, played to the crowd by tipping his cap when the booing started during pregame introductions.

■ Besides helping to calm down starter Jon Garland, the big first inning also boosted the club's confidence in a place where it had not played well. Going into the game, the White Sox had lost 15 of their previous 20 at Anaheim.

"You're able to (relax) when one team jumps out front," Angels manager Mike Scioscia said. "They were able to do that. Jon relaxed and pitched a good game."

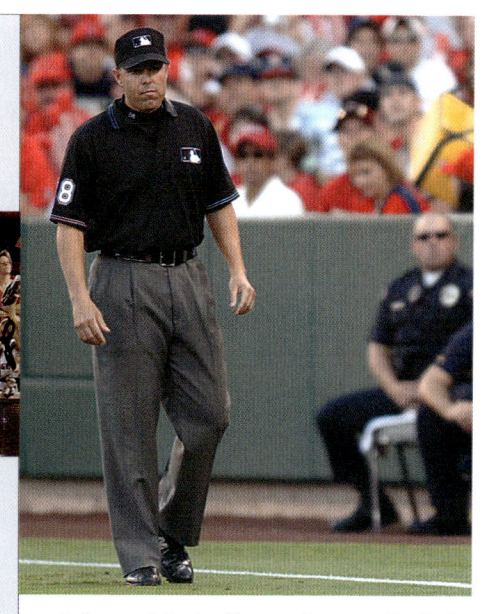

Not surprisingly, the umpires, particularly Doug Eddings, received a rough welcome at Angel Stadium during Game 3. Eddings (above) worked the right field line with security stationed nearby.

GAME 4 — A.L. CHAMPIONSHIP

WHITE SOX 8, ANGELS 2

CHICAGO	301 110 020	8	8	1	W: GARCIA (1-0, 2.00)
LOS ANGELES	010 100 000	2	6	1	L: SANTANA (0-1, 10.38)

Garcia, Konerko use a familiar formula

Winning a pennant is not supposed to look this routine. On a Saturday night at Angel Stadium, the White Sox dialed up a repeat of the formula they had used the previous night—build a quick lead and let the starting pitcher go to work. The result was an 8-2 victory that moved the Sox within one win of the American League championship.

Also like their previous victory, the White Sox followed up their performance on the field with humble talk in the clubhouse.

"We are not the type of team that is cocky. I always tell my guys, whatever happened tonight doesn't mean anything tomorrow," White Sox manager Ozzie Guillen said. "It'll be a different ballgame. When you play a short series, anything can happen."

Well, the same things keep happening for the White Sox. For the second straight game, they jumped to a 3-0 first-inning lead on the strength of a home run by Paul Konerko. And for the third straight game, their starting pitcher worked all nine innings. This time the man on the mound was righthander Freddy Garcia, who gave up six hits and walked only one while striking out five.

Scott Podsednik led off the game by working Angels starter Ervin Santana for an eight-pitch walk.

After Paul Konerko hit another first-inning homer (far right) and gave the Sox a 3-0 lead, Freddy Garcia (34) gave them another complete-game victory—and a three-games-to-one edge in the ALCS.

78 THE PRIDE OF CHICAGO

SERIES

October 15, Angel Stadium

GAME 4
2005 A.L. CHAMPIONSHIP SERIES

GARCIA: 9 IP, 6 H, 2 R, 1 BB, 5 SO

As White Sox pitchers continued their domination, Angels (left to right) Orlando Cabrera, Garret Anderson and Chone Figgins were showing the frustration of a dwindling window of opportunity.

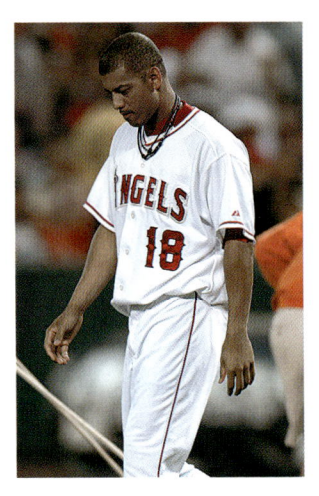

After Tadahito Iguchi was hit by a pitch, Jermaine Dye flied out. Konerko then crushed his three-run homer to left-center field—going one better than his two-run first-inning homer the day before. Konerko wasn't the only hitting star for the White Sox. Designated hitter Carl Everett delivered two-out RBI singles in the third and fifth, A.J. Pierzynski hit a homer in the fourth and Joe Crede added a two-run single in the eighth as the Sox enjoyed their highest scoring game since beating the Red Sox, 14-2, in the Division Series opener.

Garcia encountered his only real difficulty in the second when he walked Darin Erstad and made a wild throw to first after fielding a ground ball by Casey Kotchman. That put runners on second and third with one out, and the Angels scored on a single by Bengie Molina. Garcia, however, caught a break when Steve Finley grounded into a disputed double play. Finley claimed—and replays backed him up—that his swing was interfered with by A.J. Pierzynski's mitt, but no call was made. On his way to first, Finley glanced back at the home plate umpire and that probably prevented him from reaching first

What little offense the Angels did muster came with help from Freddy Garcia (34), who fielded Casey Kotchman's second-inning grounder and threw over the head of first baseman Paul Konerko (far right).

80   THE PRIDE OF CHICAGO

The Angels' second-inning rally fell apart when Steve Finley grounded into an inning-ending double play on a swing that should have been called catcher's interference. Finley lost that argument and an eighth-inning race to second (above) on a fielder's choice.

safely. Instead of looking at bases loaded and one out, the Sox were out of the inning.

"We got a break," Pierzynski said.

After the Angels scored their other run on a double by Kotchman in the fourth, Garcia retired the next 10 batters. Like Mark Buehrle and Jon Garland before him, the key to Garcia's success was the ability to get his breaking ball over for strikes, especially early in the count. "They're getting strike one, and all of them have been able to use all their pitches in any situation," Pierzynski said.

Guillen, however, still saw reason to visit Garcia after a two-out single by Erstad in the ninth.

"I talked to Freddy about having enough. (I told him) 'I have a lefty ready.' And Freddy gave me the right answer: 'Do not get me out of here,' " Guillen said. "When he gave me that answer, it was just walk away and let him pitch. I think it's nice when you have four guys there you can count on."

GAME 4 — 2005 A.L. CHAMPIONSHIP SERIES

A.L. CHAMPIONSHIP SERIES, GAME 4 — 81

GAME 4
2005 A.L. CHAMPIONSHIP SERIES

PODSEDNIK: 1-for-2, 2 R, 3 BB, 3B, 2 SB

Scott Podsednik's Game 4 heroics included three walks, two stolen bases and a triple.

Podsednik steals the show

Ozzie Guillen was asked before Game 4 why his leadoff man, Scott Podsednik, had not been running the bases as aggressively as he did during the regular season, when he stole 59 bases. "Go ask him," said Guillen, who had not taken away the green light Podsednik had all season.

There was no reason to ask after Podsednik's performance in Game 4. The White Sox left fielder walked three times, tripled, scored two runs and, yes, he stole two bases.

"We wanted to try to get to them early," said Podsednik, who led off the game with a walk and scored on Paul Konerko's three-run homer. "We wanted to try and pick up where we left off (in Game 3), put some pressure on early."

Podsednik's night was helped by an umpire's call in the fifth. Angels reliever Scot Shields appeared to have picked Podsednik off first but he was ruled safe. He then stole second and scored on a single by Carl Everett.

"Umpire called me safe," said Podsednik, with a hint of a smile.

82 THE PRIDE OF CHICAGO

Also getting in on the action were second baseman Tadahito Iguchi (15), who scored after being hit by a first-inning pitch, and right fielder Jermaine Dye (23), who stole second in the third inning and later scored.

Catcher A.J. Pierzynski contributed a home run and Carl Everett delivered a pair of two-out RBI hits as the Sox moved within one win of their first World Series since 1959.

A.L. CHAMPIONSHIP SERIES, GAME 4   83

GAME 5 — A.L. CHAMPIONSHIP
WHITE SOX 6, ANGELS 3

```
CHICAGO      010 010 112   6 8 1   W: CONTRERAS (1-1, 3.12)
LOS ANGELES  001 020 000   3 5 2   L: ESCOBAR (0-2, 2.08)
```

Opportunistic Sox ease their postseason pain

Paul Konerko fielded the grounder, stepped on first base and, just like that, the White Sox were on their way to the World Series. Forget about that near collapse in September. Forget about all those years without making the postseason, much less winning a series. And please, for once, forget about the Sox's more popular neighbors to the north. The White Sox, not the Cubs, would be representing Chicago in a fall classic for the first time in 46 years.

A 6-3 victory over the Angels on a drizzly Sunday night in Southern California sealed the deal.

"I know people are going wild right now. Chicago fans should feel real proud," White Sox manager Ozzie Guillen said. "There's 25, 30 people who helped me to win this. Those guys played hard every day, they never backed up and I think we did it for them."

The White Sox finished off their five-game ALCS victory with another complete game and more clutch hitting. Righthander Jose Contreras, the man on the mound for the Sox's fourth consecutive complete-game victory, limited the Angels to five hits and two walks. Third baseman Joe Crede delivered the big hits, tying the game with a home run in the seventh and driving in the go-ahead run in the eighth.

The victory would not have been complete without another controversial play involving Sox catcher A.J. Pierzynski—this time in the unusual role of baserunner with the score tied 3-3 in the eighth inning. With two out and Aaron Rowand on first, Pierzynski hit a bouncer that hit reliever Kelvim Escobar in the back. As Pierzynski charged toward

84 THE PRIDE OF CHICAGO

SERIES

October 16, Angel Stadium

After the final out of the ALCS was recorded, a Paul Konerko-Jose Contreras victory hug (top left) triggered a wild celebration. And why not? The White Sox were World Series-bound for the first time since 1959.

A.L. CHAMPIONSHIP SERIES, GAME 5   **85**

GAME 5 — 2005 A.L. CHAMPIONSHIP SERIES

CREDE: 2-for-3, HR, 3 RBIs

first, Escobar picked up the ball with his right hand between the mound and the first base line and tagged Pierzynski—with his glove. Realizing what he'd done, Escobar threw to first base too late. Still, Pierzynski was called out ... momentarily. Guillen raced out to argue and after the umpires assembled, the call was changed. That put runners on first and second for Crede, who bounced a single up the middle off closer Francisco Rodriguez, scoring Rowand.

The White Sox padded their lead in the ninth on an RBI double by Konerko and Rowand's sacrifice fly. Contreras retired the Angels in order in the bottom of the inning, coaxing a grounder to first by Casey Kotchman for the final out.

Like they had done in the previous two games at Angel Stadium, the White Sox took an early lead. Rowand led off the second with a double to right, moved to third on a sacrifice by Pierzynski and scored on Crede's sacrifice fly. The Angels tied the game in the third on Adam Kennedy's single, but a double by Jermaine Dye scored Juan Uribe in the fifth to put the White Sox back on top. After giving up two runs in the fifth, Contreras found his groove. He retired the last 12 Angels he faced, setting the stage for a White Sox comeback that returned the World Series to Chicago for the first time since 1959.

86 THE PRIDE OF CHICAGO

After an eighth-inning conference between pitching coach Bud Black and Kelvim Escobar (far left), the Angels pitcher fielded A.J. Pierzynski's roller and tagged him with his glove while holding the ball in his hand. When Pierzynski (12) was called out, he protested, as did Sox manager Ozzie Guillen (top center). The umpires conferred and changed the call, sparking an argument with Angels manager Mike Scioscia (top right) and a pitching change to Francisco Rodriguez (above). When the dust finally settled, Joe Crede (24) singled home the go-ahead run.

A.L. CHAMPIONSHIP SERIES, GAME 5   **87**

GAME 5 — 2005 A.L. CHAMPIONSHIP SERIES

DYE: 2-for-4, 1 R, 1 BB, 1 RBI

Angels fans had that rainy day feeling as Jose Contreras (right) fired a five-hitter and Scott Podsednik (22) returned to his base-stealing ways.

White Sox complete their journey

In 2004, one complete game was pitched in the entire postseason. In the 2005 American League Championship Series, the White Sox pitched four complete games in a row, a feat that had not been accomplished in the postseason since the 1956 Yankees. The White Sox's bullpen was called on to get only two outs in the five-game ALCS.

GAME 2: Mark Buehrle. The lefty gave up a fifth-inning homer to Robb Quinlan, but not much else. Still, he was not in line for the victory until the White Sox broke a 1-1 tie in a crazy bottom of the ninth.

GAME 3: Jon Garland. By the time he gave up a two-run homer to Orlando Cabrera in the sixth, the White Sox had a 5-0 lead. Garland allowed only four hits and walked one in his fourth complete game of the season, tying Buehrle for the team lead.

GAME 4: Freddy Garcia. Like Garland the night before, Garcia also was staked to a three-run lead in the first. He gave up runs in the second and fourth but after that, nothing. He allowed only one baserunner after the fourth inning, retiring 16 of the final 17 Angels he faced.

GAME 5: Jose Contreras. Contreras suffered the loss in Game 1 but came back to limit the Angels to five hits in the finale. "You might call it lucky, you might call it great, but we stepped up, and I'm glad I got to be part of this," Contreras said.

88 THE PRIDE OF CHICAGO

Tadahito Iguchi was hit by a first-inning pitch from Paul Byrd (left) and thrown out—almost—on an attempted steal in the ninth (below). When second baseman Adam Kennedy mishandled the on-time throw, Iguchi was called safe.

A.L. CHAMPIONSHIP SERIES, GAME 5

GAME 5 — 2005 A.L. CHAMPIONSHIP SERIES

CONTRERAS: 9 IP, 5 H, 3 R, 2 SO

Champagne was popping and spirits were high as the Sox celebrated their surprisingly easy five-game ALCS win over the Angels.

THE PRIDE OF CHICAGO

A.L. CHAMPIONSHIP SERIES, GAME 5

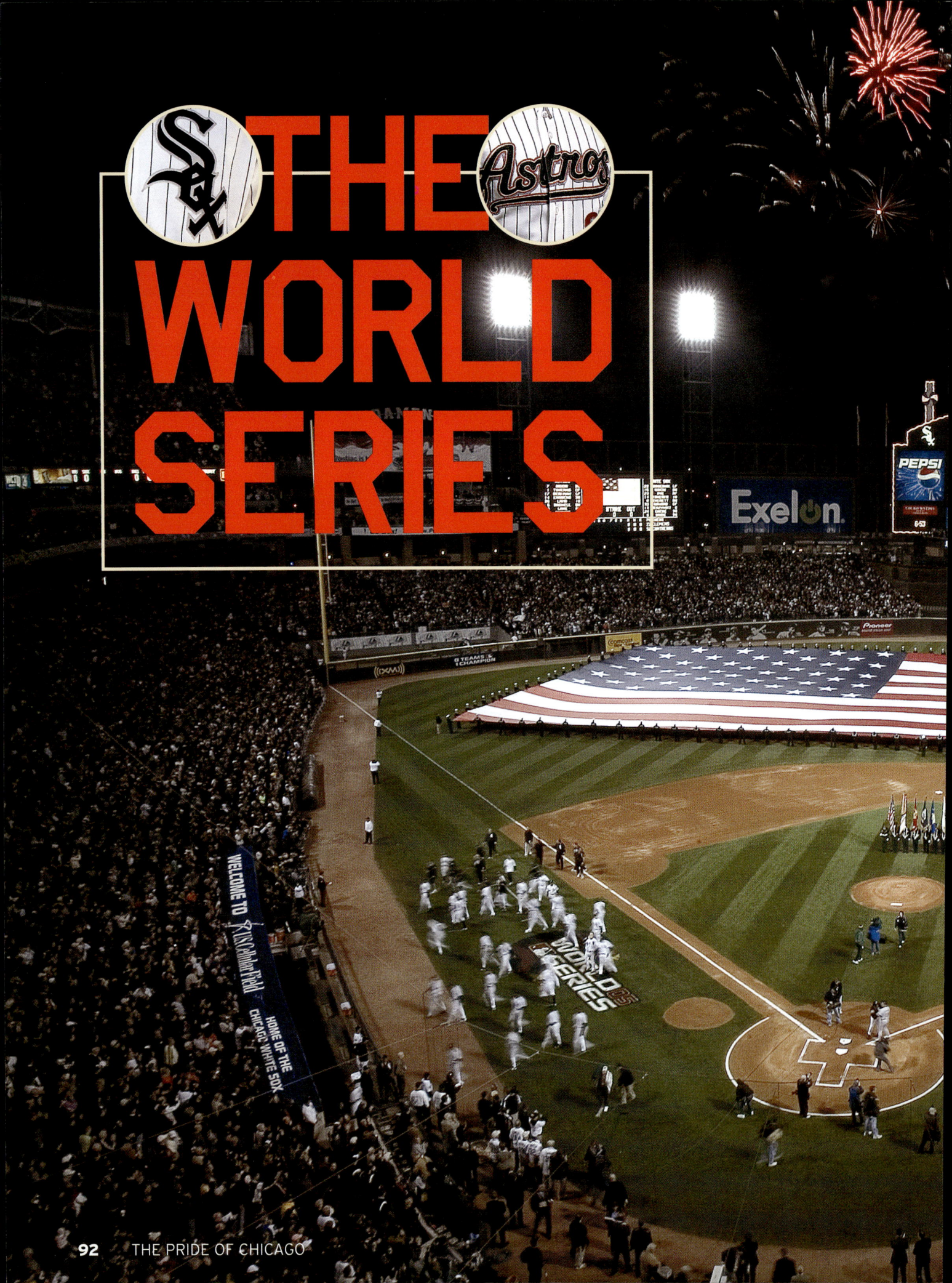

THE WORLD SERIES

92 THE PRIDE OF CHICAGO

WORLD SERIES 93

By Dave Kindred

Sox fans have baseball;

Such a thing, the World Series in Chicago. So early on the day of Game 1, I told the taxi driver, "Wrigley Field, please."

They last played the World Series at Wrigley Field two months after rookie president Harry Truman ordered atomic bombs dropped on Japan. They weren't playing at Wrigley this time, either,

While Wrigley Field hunkered down for a lonely winter, U.S. Cellular Field on Chicago's South Side hustled and bustled through a busy

THE PRIDE OF CHICAGO

Cubs fans have beer

but it seemed an act of callous disregard to be in town for the fall classic and not pay my respects to the pretty little bandbox.

And if I could annoy some Cubs fans by mentioning the White Sox, so much the better.

It didn't take long. The taxi let me out at the corner of Sheffield Avenue and Addison Street, next to the statue of Harry Caray, where I

October that produced the first White Sox World Series appearance since 1959.

WORLD SERIES 95

I took the Red Line train the 10 miles south from Wrigley to Cellular. I moved from the silence of long suffering to the cacophony of a World Series.

found four college freshmen on a road trip from Ball State University, four hours southeast.

"I know one Sox fan," said Adam Dorner. "I don't get along with him."

"One?" I said.

"Yeah," he said. His tone suggested one was far too many.

"What's the problem with him?"

"His attitude. Heard too much from him this year."

Alexander Newman, Jeff Olson and Gabriel Amick had no plans to endanger themselves by trekking to U.S. Cellular Field. "We drove by it last night," Amick said. "There weren't any gunshots, so we waved and went on."

On Addison, a man on a bicycle watched construction of an 1,800-seat addition to Wrigley's bleachers. He wore a Cubs cap. I had identified myself, taken his name, age, hometown and asked how long he'd suffered. Then Tom Rutherford, 58, Chicago, forever, said, "What are you in town for?"

"Uh, the World Series," I said.

Rutherford laughed. Of course. "Only a Cubs fan would ask that."

He predicted a historic year in 2006. The White Sox and Cubs will meet in the World Series on the centennial anniversary of "the greatest tragedy this city has ever known."

Mrs. O'Leary's cow started a fire that destroyed Chicago in 1871. It wasn't that. "In 1906," Rutherford said, "the Cubs set the all-time record for victories, 116. Then they lost the World Series to the 'hitless wonder' White Sox in six games."

At Addison and Clark streets, near a Cubs memorabilia stand, a brave man, Jim Koch, wore a White Sox cap. He's an attorney, 54, who lives near Wrigley because he likes the neighborhood. He just doesn't like the Cubs.

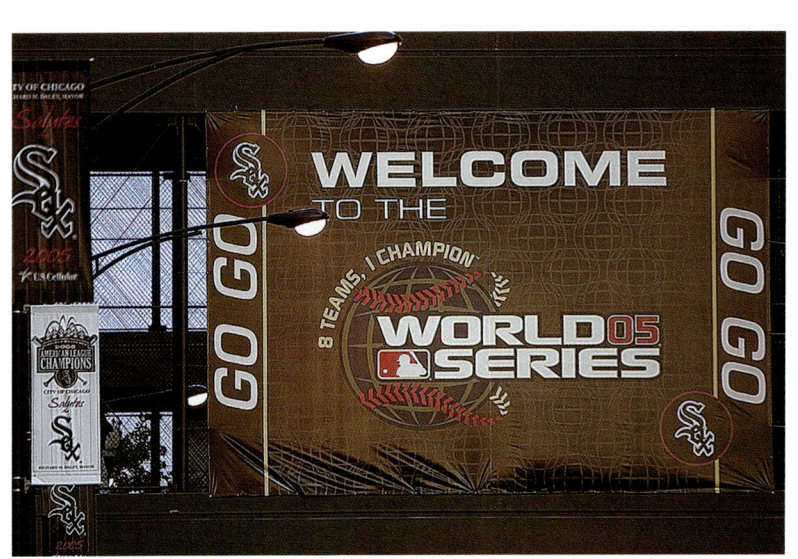

My mother is a Cubs fan, so I have to be careful. But I can say that many people believe Cubs fans are supercilious, morally pretentious, condescending elitists, not to mention snobs. As it happens, Koch has an explanation for why Wrigley is always sold out and Cellular isn't. It's not a love of the game. It's not homage to Ernie Banks. It's beer.

The attorney argues that Cubs fans could care less about baseball. All they need is enough Budweiser to float the Sears Tower off its pilings. "There are as many hard-core Sox fans as there are hard-core Cubs fans," Koch said. "The difference is, Wrigley Field is the largest saloon in the world."

I took the Red Line train the 10 miles south from Wrigley to Cellular. I moved from the silence of long suffering to the cacophony of a World Series. Not that the White Sox themselves have made the fall classic a habit. They last appeared in 1959 after 40 years of wandering in the desert of Black Sox shame. They last won one in 1917.

Shortly after 10 o'clock that night, White Sox manager Ozzie Guillen signaled for his closer. He moved his hands wide apart, as if measuring a refrigerator. Bobby Jenks is 6-3 and 270 pounds. He is a hitter's nightmare. He throws bullets and only sometimes knows where they're going. In his first 151 2/3 innings in pro baseball, Jenks struck out 140 hitters. He also walked 108, hit 17 and threw 32 wild pitches.

That was four years ago. Now a 24-year-old rookie called up from Class AA this summer, Jenks was closing in a World Series. With a one-run lead in the eighth inning, with Astros on second and third, Jenks faced Jeff Bagwell, maybe the greatest hitter in

96 THE PRIDE OF CHICAGO

Houston history. Yes, Bagwell is playing hurt. Still, he's Jeff Bagwell.

As to what Jenks threw, Bagwell said, "Gas."

The radar gun quivered at 100 mph.

On the sixth pitch, his third swing, Bagwell struck out.

"A cutter, high," he said of the killing pitch. Gas moving up and away. "Give me 500 at-bats, I don't hit that."

That game, the Sox won. Three more like it and they uncorked the champagne. Cubs fans had only their beer to cry in.

The 2005 baseball season belonged to Chicago's South Siders, who gloated, celebrated and smiled all the way to their long-awaited World Series. On the North Side, the fans pleaded (left) for something positive.

WORLD SERIES 97

GAME 1

WORLD SERIES
WHITE SOX 5, ASTROS 3

```
HOUSTON   012 000 000   3  7 1   L: RODRIGUEZ (0-1, 2.70)
CHICAGO   120 100 01x   5 10 0   W: CONTRERAS (1-0, 3.86)
```

Well-rested Sox bullpen really turns up the heat

98   THE PRIDE OF CHICAGO

October 22, U.S. Cellular Field

Impossible, it seemed. For two innings, clutching a slim lead in the first game of the World Series on their home turf, the White Sox had danced out of the way of several Astros bullets. There was a leadoff double in the sixth, which starter Jose Contreras pitched around by inducing three ground-ball outs. There were two hit batsmen in the seventh that gave the Astros a first-and-third situation, but third baseman Joe Crede's brilliant diving stop on a ground ball by Craig Biggio kept the White Sox out of trouble.

When Contreras yielded a leadoff double to Willy Taveras starting the eighth, though, it looked like the White Sox's 4-3 lead might finally melt away. That was when manager Ozzie Guillen decided to turn up the heat on a crisp and cool night at U.S. Cellular Field by turning to his bullpen, an unknown factor heading into the series. Thanks to four straight complete-game victories in the ALCS, the bullpen hadn't worked in 10 days—and had thrown just two-thirds of an inning in 15.

"We were pretty pumped up," said lefty reliever

Pure heat. First Chicago lefthander Neal Cotts (46) warmed things up with his mid-90s fastball, then closer Bobby Jenks (45) really turned up the gas. Astros star Jeff Bagwell (above) could not catch up to Jenks, who struck out three of the four batters he faced.

WORLD SERIES, GAME 1   99

GAME 1 — 2005 WORLD SERIES

CONTRERAS: 7 IP, 3 R, 0 BB, 2 SO

Jose Contreras could not match his complete-game effort in the ALCS, but he was good enough to raise his postseason record to 3-1.

Neal Cotts, who got the call from Guillen to replace Contreras. "The layoff gave us all a little extra zip."

Cotts started Lance Berkman with a slider, which Berkman knocked into left for a single. But then he turned to the zip. With runners on first and third base and none out, Cotts threw 11 straight fastballs ranging from 93-95 mph to Morgan Ensberg and Mike Lamb, and struck out both.

Not enough heat? Guillen then called on rookie closer Bobby Jenks, who started by throwing a 99-mph fastball to Jeff Bagwell, and finished by blowing a 100-mph bullet past the Astros veteran for the third strikeout of the eighth. Jenks closed the game by striking out two more hitters in a scoreless ninth.

"They weren't catching up with the fastballs, so we just kept going with them," catcher A.J. Pierzynski said. "With Neal and Bobby, that's their best pitch. Why not lean on it?"

It was a tense finish to a game that appeared to be headed toward a high score in the early innings. Houston starter Roger Clemens, dealing with a strained hamstring, left the game in the second inning after giving up a home run to Jermaine Dye in the first and two runs in the second on an RBI grounder by Pierzynski and a double by Juan Uribe. The Astros got to Contreras, too, tying the score at 3 with a run in the second on Mike Lamb's homer and two more in the third on Berkman's double.

The White Sox reclaimed the lead for Contreras in the fourth when Crede's fly ball to center field just got over the wall with some help from the October wind. Contreras settled down by using his defense—he retired seven straight batters on three grounders, three fly balls and one strikeout—and set up the heroics of Crede, Cotts and Jenks.

"That is when Jose is at his best," Pierzynski said. "When he just sits back and lets the defense do its work, keeps the ball down and gets ground balls, he is not going to give up much. It helps him when he gets into tough situations."

Doesn't hurt to have a hard-throwing bullpen, either.

100 THE PRIDE OF CHICAGO

Juan Uribe's RBI double (left) capped a two-run second-inning assault against Roger Clemens (22), who left with a hamstring injury. Clemens got a shuttle ride (below) to the locker room.

GAME **1** 2005 WORLD SERIES

WORLD SERIES, GAME 1   101

GAME 1 — 2005 WORLD SERIES

CREDE: 1-for-4, HR, 1 RBI

Crede delivers big with bat, glove

The White Sox have waited—sometimes not so patiently—for Joe Crede to become the player they envisioned when they drafted him in 1996. In Game 1 of the World Series, he gave them a tantalizing glimpse.

Crede hit the fourth-inning home run that gave the Sox a 4-3 lead over the Astros and the eventual winning run. But the game might have hinged even more on two brilliant defensive plays that left Houston frustrated and extended the Astros' disappointing offensive performance in the most crucial situations.

With a runner at third and one out in the sixth inning, Sox manager Ozzie Guillen brought the infield in, a risky move with cleanup hitter Morgan Ensberg at the plate. Ensberg hit a shot down the third base line. Crede made a diving stab, held the runner and threw out Ensberg. With runners at first and third in the next inning, he pulled the same magic on a hard Craig Biggio grounder to Crede's backhand.

"Joe is the big-hit wonder," teammate Aaron Rowand said. "But, more important is the defense. He had a couple of plays where if he doesn't make them, we lose the game. The defense is always more important to Joe."

Crede, frequently the target of fan abuse during a season in which he hit only .252, agreed. "We were playing aggressive defense," Crede said. "Any time you're not getting hits, you don't want anybody else to get hits, either. Your focus goes up that much more. I take that mentality whenever I go out on defense."

He took the Astros out as well.

The Joe Crede Show included a tiebreaking home run (top) that just cleared the glove of leaping center fielder Willy Taveras (left) and two diving backhand stops (right) that thwarted Houston rallies.

102 THE PRIDE OF CHICAGO

WORLD SERIES, GAME 1 103

GAME 1 — 2005 WORLD SERIES

Houston's first World Series game did not have a happy ending for Astros fans.

One of Chicago's two second-inning runs came when A.J. Pierzynski (right) hit a fielder's choice grounder that scored Carl Everett (below).

DYE: 1-for-2, HR, 1 RBI, 2 BB

104 THE PRIDE OF CHICAGO

When Ozzie Guillen needs his closer, he spreads his arms far apart (right) and signals for "the big boy," rookie righthander Bobby Jenks. Guillen gives Jenks some last-minute instruction (below) before turning him loose on the Astros.

GAME 1 — 2005 WORLD SERIES

WORLD SERIES, GAME 1   105

GAME 2 WORLD SERIES
WHITE SOX 7, ASTROS 6

```
HOUSTON   011 020 002   6  9 0   L: LIDGE (0-1, 27.00)
CHICAGO   020 000 401   7 12 0   W: COTTS (1-0, 0.00)
```

Podsednik homer defies Astronomical odds

Nothing in baseball is more dramatic than the walkoff home run. And when one comes in the World Series, it's truly a moment to savor. Some of the game's biggest names have ended World Series games with homers, including Mickey Mantle, Mark McGwire and Kirby Puckett. Some of the fall classic's finest moments have come courtesy of dramatic last at-bat home runs by Bill Mazeroski, Carlton Fisk, Kirk Gibson and Joe Carter.

But the 14th walkoff home run in World Series history came from the most unlikely of sources: White Sox leadoff man Scott Podsednik, who had so often ignited the team's offense with his speed. In Game 2, though, with the score tied in the bottom of the ninth, Podsednik, who had not hit a home run in 507 at-bats during the regular season, lifted Chicago to a win with a long one-out drive to right-center field off Astros closer Brad Lidge, giving the Sox a 7-6 win and a 2-0 series lead.

When it was over, Podsednik was slightly dazed and speechless. "To go out and hit one out of the ballpark for a game-winner is pretty much indescribable," he said.

For the White Sox, it was a beautiful ending to a

106 THE PRIDE OF CHICAGO

Scott Podsednik (above, left) joined the exclusive club of World Series walkoff home run hitters when he connected in the ninth inning off Astros closer Brad Lidge (far left), giving the Sox a 2-0 series advantage.

WORLD SERIES, GAME 2 **107**

GAME 2 — 2005 WORLD SERIES

Mark Buerhle (above) battled the elements and struggled through seven tough innings.

sloppy game, one slowed by a steady rain, gusting wind and temperatures that dropped into the 30s.

"Coldest game we played all year," said outfielder Jermaine Dye. "It was tough out there."

Over the first six innings, the White Sox managed eight hits, but struggled to get their bats going in the clutch, scoring just twice. Starting pitcher Mark Buehrle fought the bad weather and gave up four runs while laboring through seven innings.

KONERKO: 1-for-4, HR, 4 RBIs

108 THE PRIDE OF CHICAGO

The Astros led, 4-2, with two out in the seventh when the White Sox's fortunes changed. With Juan Uribe on second, Tadahito Iguchi drew a walk and Jermaine Dye was hit by a pitch (a controversial call, because replays showed that the ball hit Dye's bat first). That brought cleanup hitter Paul Konerko to the plate, and he did clean up, lacing the first pitch he saw from reliever Chad Qualls over the left field wall for a grand slam that gave Chicago a 6-4 lead.

"It sure looked like we had them at that point," Dye said. "We were feeling pretty good."

Down 4-2 in the seventh, the White Sox roared back when Tadahito Iguchi drew a walk (top, far left) and Jermaine Dye was hit by a pitch (far left), loading the bases. Houston reliever Chad Qualls (50) entered the game and surrendered a first-pitch grand slam to Paul Konerko (above).

GAME 2 — 2005 WORLD SERIES

WORLD SERIES, GAME 2   109

GAME 2 — 2005 WORLD SERIES

BUEHRLE: 7 IP, 4 R, 0 BB, 6 SO

But the Astros had a rally of their own in the ninth against closer Bobby Jenks. Pinch hitter Jose Vizcaino delivered the big blow, a two-out, two-run, opposite-field single that sent a shiver through the already frigid U.S. Cellular crowd. That is, until Podsednik came to the plate and worked the count to two balls and a strike. When Lidge left a fastball up in the strike zone, Podsednik's improbable homer was on the way.

"I don't think anyone in the ballpark thought I was going to hit a home run," Podsednik said. "Lucky I got in a hitter's count, I was looking for a fastball the entire count, and got one."

Whatever missed opportunities the White Sox had throughout the game were forgotten with that swing.

"This team made me mad for seven innings," said Sox manager Ozzie Guillen, "but they made me smile in the ninth."

Rain and cold were the order of the day for players as well as grounds crew members. Some players, like Astros reliever Dan Wheeler (35), had a tough time getting a grip, while others, like Chicago's Carl Everett, just soaked everything in.

110 THE PRIDE OF CHICAGO

Oh, baby, what a week for Konerko!

How's this for a week?

On Monday, having helped his team to an ALCS title while earning series MVP honors, **Paul Konerko** flew to Arizona. He spent most of Tuesday evening in the waiting-room of a hospital, pacing from time to time as his wife, Jennifer, went into labor with the couple's first child. Konerko had Wednesday to enjoy his first day of fatherhood with newborn Nicholas, then headed back to Chicago on Thursday. On Saturday he played in the first World Series game of his career.

On Sunday, he hit the 18th grand slam in World Series history.

Konerko had struggled for most of Game 2, going 0-for-3 with a strikeout before stepping in to face Chad Qualls with the bases loaded and two out in the bottom of the seventh inning. He guessed Qualls would start him with a fastball, and he guessed correctly.

"I wasn't thinking home run," Konerko said. "I was thinking base hit to drive in two runs."

But the home run came, and it was quite a capper for the most popular White Sox player, a fact that became evident when the home crowd cheered Konerko ("Paul-ie! Paul-ie!") into giving a rare curtain call after the homer.

"Not too many times," Konerko said, "are you going to hit a grand slam in a World Series game and have it be the second-best thing that happened to you in a week."

Willy Taveras (1) slides safely into third with a triple as Joe Crede scoops up the low throw and the umpire watches the action. Moments later, Taveras scored a third-inning run on a sacrifice fly.

GAME 2 2005 WORLD SERIES

WORLD SERIES, GAME 2 111

GAME 2 — 2005 WORLD SERIES

PODSEDNIK: Walkoff HR

Astros third baseman Morgan Ensberg couldn't believe it when he was called out on strikes in the third inning (above). Left fielder Chris Burke missed connections on a sixth-inning double by Aaron Rowand (left), but Astros Andy Pettitte and shortstop Adam Everett did get Juan Uribe (below) in the fifth on a fielder's choice.

112 THE PRIDE OF CHICAGO

Second baseman Craig Biggio dropped Juan Uribe's popup (above), but the Astros recovered and got a force at second as a run scored.

Down to their last out in the top of the ninth inning, Astros pinch hitter Jose Vizcaino (left) singled home two runners, including Chris Burke (above), who slid home with the tying score. The White Sox fought back in the bottom of the inning when Scott Podsednik triggered a celebration (right) with his home run.

GAME 2 — 2005 WORLD SERIES

WORLD SERIES, GAME 2

GAME 3 WORLD SERIES
WHITE SOX 7, ASTROS 5

```
CHICAGO   000 050 000 000 02   7 14 3   W: MARTE (1-0, 0.00)
HOUSTON   102 100 010 000 00   5  8 1   L: ASTACIO (0-1, 27.00)
```

Blum decides marathon with 14th

After a game that went 14 innings, lasted 5 hours and 41 minutes and set a longevity (by time) record, the White Sox woke up one victory away from winning the World Series.

Their 7-5 win, which gave them a 3-0 lead over the Houston Astros, started at 7:39 p.m. (Central time) on a Tuesday and ended at 1:20 a.m. on a Wednesday. The decisive blow came on a home run by Geoff Blum, who had not batted in three weeks. The winning pitcher, Damaso Marte, had not pitched in 18 days. The save went to Mark Buehrle, who had not worked in relief in five years.

Incredible? Indeed.

"If we win tomorrow we could win two World Series games in the same day," Blum said. "I don't think that's ever been done."

It has been, but numerous other things that happened in this game were unprecedented:

■ 30 men were left on base, 15 by each team. "We might have played 40 innings, and it didn't look like we were going to get a runner across the bag," Astros manager Phil Garner said.

■ 17 pitchers were used, nine by the White Sox. In the only other 14-inning World Series game, a 2-1 victory by the Red Sox over the Brooklyn Dodgers in 1916, only two pitchers worked: starters Babe Ruth and Sherry Smith.

■ The Sox's nine pitchers issued 12 walks, even though starter Jon Garland passed only two in seven innings. From the eighth on, eight relievers combined to allow 13 baserunners but only one hit. That was the run-scoring double by Jason Lane off Dustin Hermanson in the eighth that tied the game—the Astros' only hit after Lane's leadoff homer in the fourth.

■ 43 players were used. Backup White Sox catcher Chris Widger didn't enter the game until the bottom of the ninth but still batted three times and drove in the game's final run with a bases-loaded walk.

THE PRIDE OF CHICAGO

October 25, Minute Maid Park

-inning homer

As the ball leaves the bat of Geoff Blum in the 14th inning of Game 3, Houston's championship hopes grow dim. Blum, who had not batted in three weeks, got a warm greeting at home plate from Aaron Rowand and lifelong membership in the 'World Series Unlikely Hero Club.'

GAME 3

2005 WORLD SERIES

GARLAND: 7 IP, 2 ER, 4 SO

ASTROS PITCHERS: 8

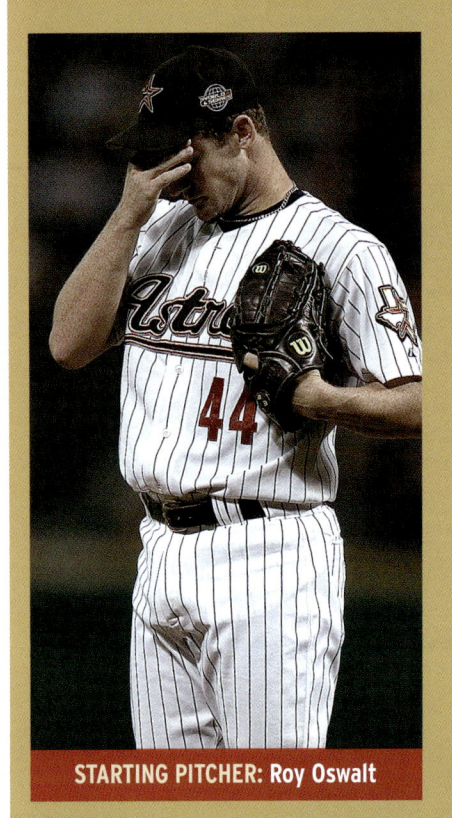

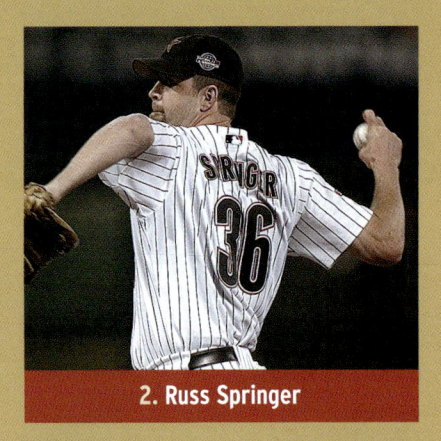

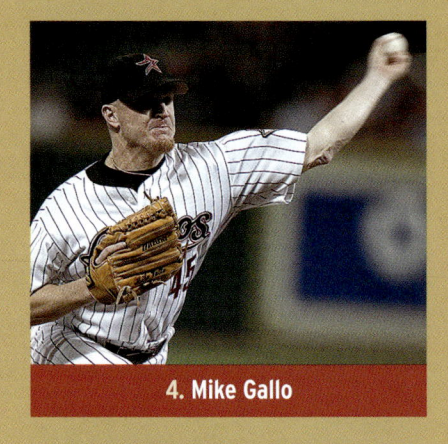

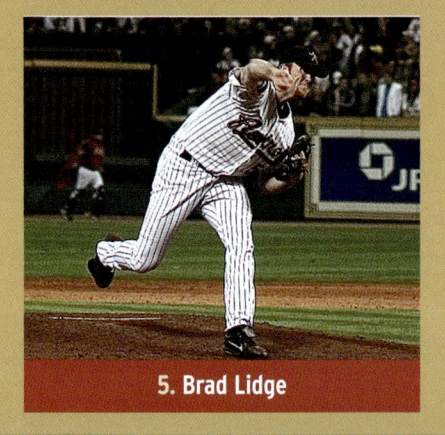

STARTING PITCHER: Roy Oswalt

2. Russ Springer

3. Dan Wheeler

4. Mike Gallo

5. Brad Lidge

WHITE SOX PITCHERS: 9

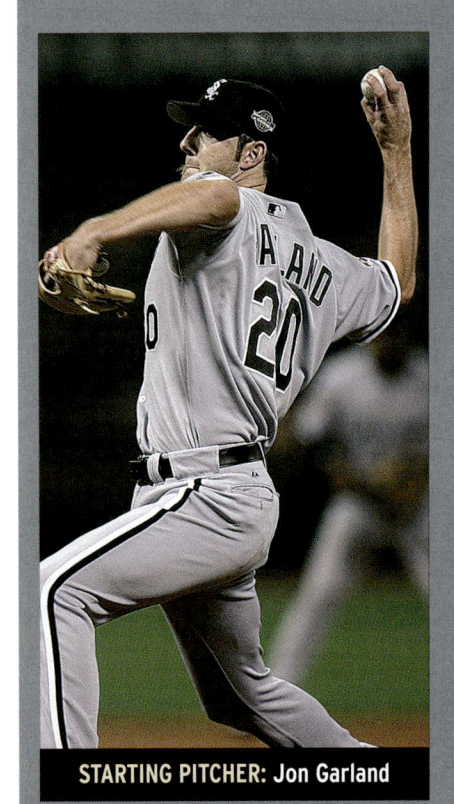

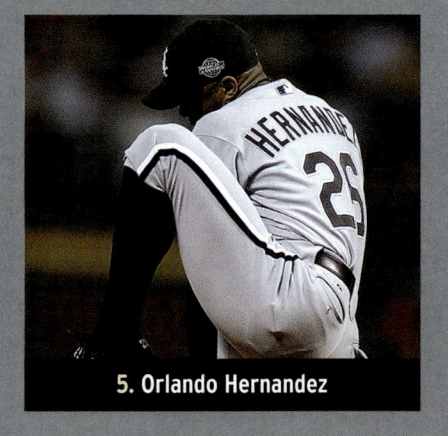

STARTING PITCHER: Jon Garland

2. Cliff Politte

3. Neal Cotts

4. Dustin Hermanson

5. Orlando Hernandez

116 THE PRIDE OF CHICAGO

17 pitchers, 14 innings

The longest game (by time) in World Series history also featured the most pitchers used by both teams. Fans saw a parade of 17 hurlers, which easily topped the previous fall classic record of 13.

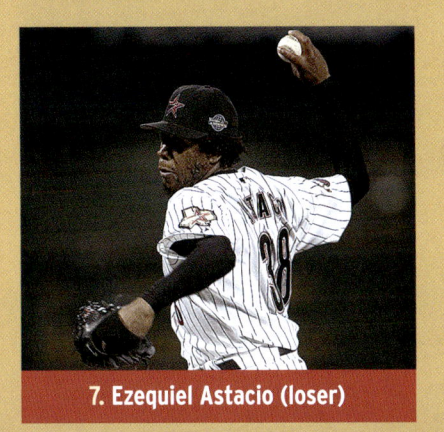

6. Chad Qualls
7. Ezequiel Astacio (loser)
8. Wandy Rodriguez 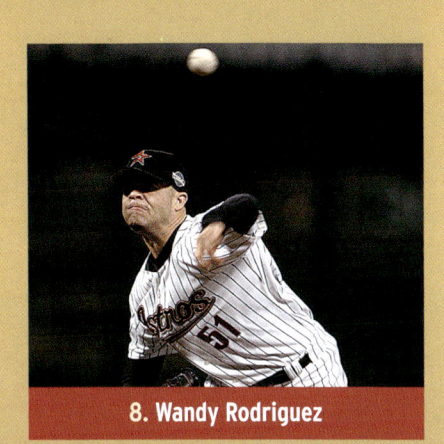
6. Luis Vizcaino 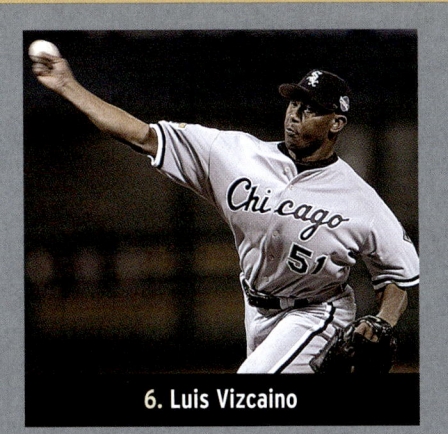
8. Damaso Marte (winner) 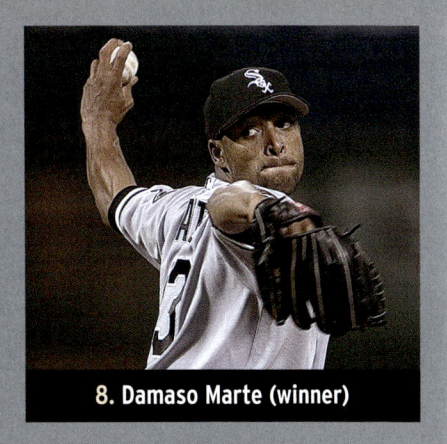
7. Bobby Jenks 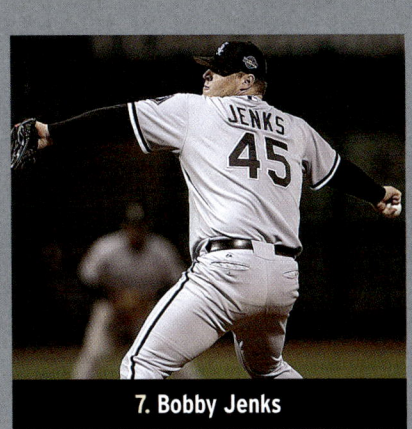
9. Mark Buehrle (save) 

"When you are managing, you just want to get the thing over with," White Sox boss Ozzie Guillen said. "Thank God (Blum) did it because I was running out of pitchers."

The game began normally enough. The Astros took advantage of early struggles by Garland, who was making only his second start of the postseason. He allowed four runs and seven hits in the first four innings before settling in and working three scoreless innings.

Astros starter Roy Oswalt, meanwhile, changed his game plan from his previous two starts in the NLCS, relying more on his breaking pitches and less on his fastball. The strategy worked for four innings as the Astros built a 4-0 lead.

Then the night turned strange. In the fifth, Oswalt gave up five runs and six hits—he had allowed only five runs combined in his previous three postseason starts. The righthander threw 46 pitches in the inning, a career high. Perhaps most surprising: Garner sent Oswalt out for the sixth, and he made it through with no problems.

"He was a little wild (in the fifth)," Guillen said. "This kid can shut them down real quick because he's that good. We execute—we approach real well—against him."

Joe Crede started the fifth inning with a home run. The White Sox scored two more times on singles from four of their next five batters—Juan Uribe, Scott Podsednik, Tadahito Iguchi and Jermaine Dye. After Paul Konerko flied out, A.J. Pierzynski delivered a two-out, two-run double that put the White Sox in front. "A.J. was the key," Guillen said.

"Dye's at-bat was critical," Garner disagreed. "(Roy) pitched in a really good sequence and Dye flipped the ball out in center field. They just got some hits, that's what they've been doing in this series."

Then the Sox went nine innings before scoring again. Dye led off the 14th with a single but promptly was doubled up when third baseman Morgan Ensberg picked off a hard grounder by Konerko. Just when it

GAME **3** 2005 WORLD SERIES

WORLD SERIES, GAME 3   117

GAME 3 — 2005 WORLD SERIES

seemed like rookie Ezequiel Astacio would make it through his first inning with the game still tied, Blum deposited a 2-0 fastball into the right field seats. A rattled Astacio allowed the next four Sox to reach base, walking Widger to force in a run that gave the Sox a two-run cushion.

The Astros put two runners on in their half of the 14th against Marte before Buehrle entered with two out and got Adam Everett to pop out. That put the White Sox one win away from their first World Series championship in 88 years.

Joe Crede's home run (below) got Chicago on the board in the fifth inning, while Geoff Blum's 14th-inning shot, which eluded Astros right fielder Jason Lane (below right), decided the game.

Minute Maid Park's roof stayed open for Houston's first World Series game, negating the noisier home-field advantage the Astros could have enjoyed.

BLUM: 1-for-1, 1R, HR, 1 RBI

118 THE PRIDE OF CHICAGO

The most unlikely of heroes

To say Geoff Blum was an unlikely hero would be like saying Ozzie Guillen likes to talk a little. Yes, an understatement.

To begin with, Blum spent the 2002 and '03 seasons with the team his 14th-inning home run defeated and deflated. The seven-year veteran did not join the White Sox until the trade deadline this summer when he was sent over from the Padres for—pay attention, this could be the answer to a trivia question some day—minor league pitcher Ryan Meaux.

After the White Sox acquired Blum to fill a utility role, he hit one homer and batted .200 while appearing in 31 games. Blum had not driven in a run in 56 days and had not even played since the first game of the postseason.

So it was no surprise when he went to the plate thinking he would take a pitch or two. "The first pitch definitely was taken because I hadn't seen a pitch in three or four weeks," he said.

"I wanted to gauge the velocity a little bit, see if I was seeing one ball or three."

After getting ahead in the count 2-0, Blum had seen enough. Astros righthander Ezequiel Astacio threw a fastball just like Blum was expecting. The result was a home run that decided Game 3 and, really, the World Series.

"I took a chance and fortunately he got the ball up," Blum said. "As soon as I hit it, I knew it was high enough to get out. As soon as it got out, (first base coach) Tim Raines' face lit up and he stuck his hand up. Hitting his hand and touching the base was a little tough.

"It's the stuff dreams are made of. I've had about a hundred of these at-bats in my backyard with my younger brother. But to do it on this stage and in this situation makes this year incredibly worthwhile."

White Sox fans will say that, too, is a bit of an understatement.

GAME 3 — 2005 WORLD SERIES

CREDE: 2-for-5, HR, 1 RBI

Other contributors to the 14-inning win were Scott Podsednik (22), who had two hits and stole a base; A.J. Pierzynski (12), who delivered a two-run double in the fifth; and defenders Juan Uribe (5) and Tadahito Iguchi (15).

120 THE PRIDE OF CHICAGO

An unusual numbers game

A game this unusual is sure to produce some unusual numbers:

0 The number of runs allowed by closers Bobby Jenks and Brad Lidge. Both had problems in Game 2, but both were back in form for Game 3. Lidge retired all four batters he faced, three on strikeouts. Jenks allowed two baserunners—a walk and hit batsman—in his two innings and struck out three.

1 The number of people in the White Sox dugout who called Geoff Blum's 14th-inning homer run. It was Oney Guillen, Ozzie's son. Ozzie explains: "Before that game starts, my kid next to me said, 'Blum is going to win it for you.' I looked at him and he gave me a bad look. When he hit the home run, you can see TV, when he's making fun of me. He called that shot."

6 The approximate number of inches by which umpires missed a call on Jason Lane's fourth-inning homer. The ball actually landed about half a foot to the left of the home run line and should have been in play. It was one of the few times a call had gone against the White Sox in the postseason.

28 The number of pitches thrown by Orlando "El Duque" Hernandez in the ninth inning. He walked three and allowed Chris Burke to reach third with one out but did not give up a run. He struck out Morgan Ensberg with the bases loaded to end the inning. Hernandez walked Orlando Palmeiro to open the 10th inning but was unable to continue because of tightness in his neck.

47 The number of times the Astros went to the plate after Jason Lane led off the fourth inning wiith a home run. They had one hit, an RBI single by Lane that tied the game in the eighth.

50 The difference, in minutes, between the time of this game (5:41) and the next longest World Series game. Game 1 of the Subway Series in 2000 took 4 hours and 51 minutes. The only other 14-inning World Series game—played in 1916 between the Red Sox and Dodgers—lasted 2 hours, 32 minutes.

61 The temperature (in degrees) at game time at Minute Maid Park. Because of the cool evening, the major league office ruled that the roof would have to be open for the game. That was not good news for the Astros, who had gone 42-18 through the regular season and Game 2 of the World Series with the roof closed, 15-11 with it open.

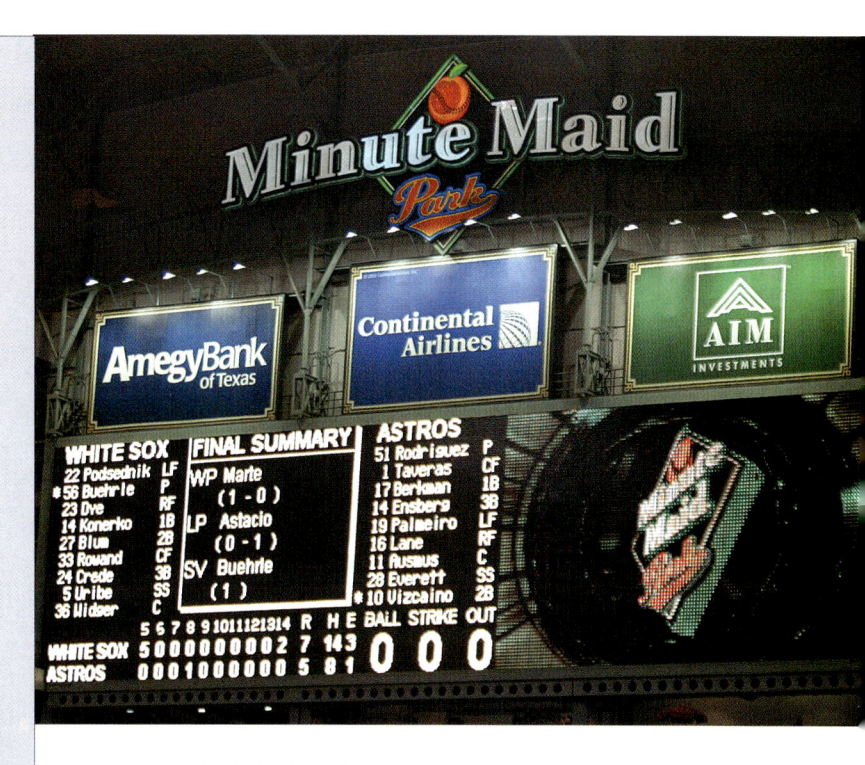

The overworked Minute Maid Park scoreboard tells the final story of Chicago's 14-inning victory. Before Geoff Blum's homer in the 14th, right fielder Jermaine Dye (23) had been the last White Sox player to cross the plate—in the fifth inning.

GAME **3** 2005 WORLD SERIES

WORLD SERIES, GAME 3   121

GAME 4

WORLD SERIES
WHITE SOX 1, ASTROS 0

```
CHICAGO   000 000 010   1 8 0   W: GARCIA (1-0, 0.00)
HOUSTON   000 000 000   0 5 0   L: LIDGE (0-2, 4.91)
```

THE DROUGHT ENDS:
Sox clinch their first championship since 1917

Na na na na, na na na na, hey hey, goodbye!

That catchy ditty, which blares at U.S. Cellular Field whenever an opponent has been defeated, could be queued up for another reason after the White Sox's 1-0 victory in Game 4 of the 2005 World Series: Goodbye frustration. See ya later 88 years of coming up short.

Ozzie Guillen's guys clinched the White Sox's first championship since 1917 with a formula that typified their season: excellent pitching, outstanding defense, just enough hitting and flawless button-pushing by the manager.

"It's a great feeling," Guillen said. "Chicago has waited so long and had so much patience, and are still there for us, rooting for us. A good thing happened to us. With the birth of my kids, this is the

When Juan Uribe's throw retired Orlando Palmeiro for the final out of the World Series, the White Sox began their obligatory on-field celebration, starting with a Bobby Jenks-A.J. Pierzynski hug (left) and the traditional group squeeze.

122 THE PRIDE OF CHICAGO

October 26, Minute Maid Park

GAME 4 — 2005 WORLD SERIES

GARCIA: 7 IP, 0 R, 3 BB, 7 SO

124   THE PRIDE OF CHICAGO

most wonderful day of my life."

Like the first three games of the Series, Game 4 was tight to the final out. The difference this time was the team balance of the White Sox.

The offense: In a game dominated for seven innings by Freddy Garcia and Astros starter Brandon Backe, the White Sox pulled a page out of the Ozzie Ball handbook to scratch across a run off Brad Lidge in the eighth. Willie Harris, who had not batted since the first game of the A.L. Division Series, was called on by Guillen to pinch hit leading off the inning and came through with a two-strike single to left. He was sacrificed to second by Scott Podsednik and moved to third on a grounder to second by pinch hitter Carl Everett. Jermaine Dye, who already had two hits, bounced a 1-1 slider up the middle to bring in Harris.

"I know he throws a lot of sliders," said Dye, the Series MVP. "I stuck with the game plan of

Bobby Jenks threw up his arms when the final out was recorded, but the real celebration took place in the locker room, where White Sox owner Jerry Reinsdorf (above) accepted the World Series trophy he long had craved.

WORLD SERIES, GAME 4   125

GAME 4 — 2005 WORLD SERIES

DYE: 3-for-4, 2B, 1 RBI

going up there, looking for a slider and not trying to do too much with it. I just tried to hit it hard and found a hole up the middle."

The pitching: Garcia, coming off a complete-game victory in the ALCS, was on from the start. He gave up four hits and allowed only one Astros player to reach third base. Garcia struck out seven before giving way to the bullpen. The trio of Cliff Politte, Neal Cotts and Bobby Jenks finished the shutout with a gutty run through the Astros' lineup. The Astros put two runners on in the eighth and led off the ninth with a single but were unable to crack the Sox with a clutch hit.

The defense: One reason the Astros couldn't come through with a big hit in the final innings was the play of shortstop Juan

The White Sox were not without fans in Houston, including Steve Perry (above), the rock star who wrote "Don't Stop Believin'," the unofficial White Sox theme song. Left to mourn the Astros' missed opportunity were Houston's First Couple (left)—former president George Bush and wife Barbara.

THE PRIDE OF CHICAGO

D-Y-E is as simple as M-V-P

A case for World Series Most Valuable Player honors could have been made for several White Sox players. And if managers were eligible, Ozzie Guillen would have been a great choice. Every move he made seemed to work. Among the players, Joe Crede hit two home runs and sparkled at third base. Scott Podsednik provided a spark at the top of the order and won Game 2 with a dramatic walkoff homer. Paul Konerko led the team with four RBIs. A.J. Pierzynski, as usual, was in the middle of everything. And rookie Bobby Jenks saved three of the four victories.

Dye led all Sox players in the Series with seven hits, a .438 average and a .526 on-base percentage.

All worthy of consideration. But no one could dispute the worthiness of the guy who did win the award—right fielder Jermaine Dye. In his first year with the White Sox after signing as a free agent, Dye drove in the only run in the Series clincher with a two-out, eighth-inning single off Astros closer Brad Lidge.

But that's not all he did. Dye homered in his first at-bat of the Series to get the White Sox off on the right foot. He led all players with seven hits and a .438 average. He reached base at least twice in all four games and posted a .526 on-base percentage.

And, true to his low-key personality, he remained humble in the wake of his achievements.

"We all worked hard to do whatever we could to help this team win and guys came up with big hits in a lot of situations," he said. "It's just special for me to be thought of as an MVP and become an MVP in that group."

When Dye, 31, was being pursued as a free agent last winter, he chose the White Sox, even though other teams offered him a better contract. He did not want to go back to a team in the West. He liked the Midwest because of an easier travel schedule. He liked the A.L. Central Division because he was familiar with it from his time with the Royals. And, oh yes, he liked the White Sox's chances of being a good team.

"I sat down and looked at, first of all, what kind of pitching staff we had, because in order to win and get to the playoffs you need to have pitchers," Dye said. "This team is built around pitching and defense. And these guys have been doing it the whole year."

So did Dye, who hit 31 homers in the regular season but saved his biggest hits for October.

Jermaine Dye, who drove in the Series-clinching run, gets a victory lift from Carl Everett.

GAME 4 — 2005 WORLD SERIES

WORLD SERIES, GAME 4   127

GAME 4
2005 WORLD SERIES

128 THE PRIDE OF CHICAGO

Uribe, who came up with three highlight plays in the eighth and ninth.

With two out and a runner on third in the eighth, Uribe barehanded a slow roller and fired to first in time to retire pinch hitter Jose Vizcaino by half a step. After Jason Lane singled and moved to second on a sacrifice in the ninth, Uribe tumbled head-first into the stands behind third base after ranging far into foul ground to snare a pop by pinch hitter Chris Burke. On the next play, another pinch hitter, Orlando Palmeiro, hit a bouncer over Jenks that Uribe fielded on the run in front of second and made another strong throw to first just in time to get the out—and clinch the White Sox victory.

It completed a run during which Chicago left no doubt this was baseball's best team in 2005. The Sox won 16 of their last 17 games going back to the regular season, and their 11-1 record in the postseason matched the 1999 Yankees for best postseason record since the introduction of the wild card.

"I told my players the last 11 games we have to win are the toughest ones," said Guillen. Guillen also had told his players, after they clinched the A.L. Central Division, that they would go into Cleveland and sweep the Indians in the season's final weekend. They did just that, then followed up by dominating the Red Sox 3-0, beating the Angels 4-1 and sweeping the Astros.

And in so doing, they bid farewell to an 88-year drought.

Na na na na, na na na na, hey hey, goodbye!

It was small ball at its best, just like manager Ozzie Guillen wanted to see it executed. With Astros closer Brad Lidge (top, far left) on the mound in the eighth inning, Scott Podsednik bunted the runner to second, Jermaine Dye delivered a two-out single and Willie Harris scored (left) the game's only run.

GAME 4 — 2005 WORLD SERIES

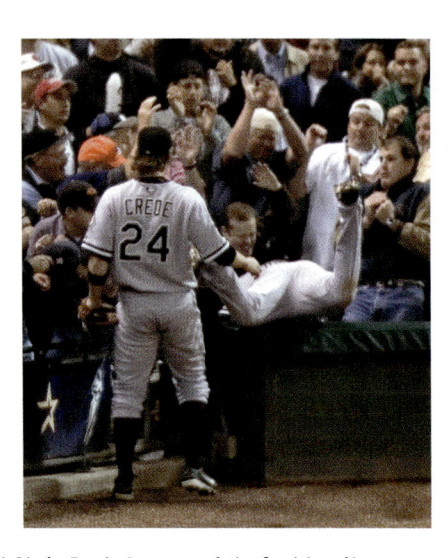

A big ninth-inning defensive boost was provided by shortstop Juan Uribe (5), who chased Chris Burke's popup into foul territory behind third base and lunged to make the catch, holding onto the ball as he tumbled into the stands.

JENKS: 1 IP, 1 H, Save

Neither team blinked over the first seven innings, which featured a pitching duel between Freddy Garcia (34) and the Astros' Brandon Backe. Garcia allowed only four hits, Backe five.

130 THE PRIDE OF CHICAGO

It was that kind of a night for Astros slugger Lance Berkman (far left), who watched third baseman Joe Crede (left), second baseman Tadahito Iguchi (below) and all the White Sox defenders make every play they needed to make.

One of the few early scoring threats came on Scott Podsednik's two-out triple in the third inning, but he was stranded.

GAME 4 2005 WORLD SERIES

WORLD SERIES, GAME 4 131

GAME 4 | 2005 WORLD SERIES

HARRIS: 1-for-1, 1 R

132 THE PRIDE OF CHICAGO

Pitcher Mark Buehrle shares some of the celebratory champagne with White Sox fans who made the happy trip to Houston.

GAME 4 2005 WORLD SERIES

WORLD SERIES, GAME 4 133

2005 WORLD SERIES

Two days after watching their Sox wrap up the World Series title, Chicagoans celebrated with a ticker-tape parade through the downtown streets of the city.

134 THE PRIDE OF CHICAGO

3324
3323
LEE #59
DYE #23
GARCIA #34
ANDERSON #44
MARTE #43
BAINES #3
GARLAND #20
PEREZ #7
CHICAGO DOUBLE DECKER CO.

By Dave Kindred

Good old country HARDBALL

Game 4, bottom of the sixth, no score, bases loaded, two out, 0-2 count, and here comes White Sox pitcher Freddy Garcia with a breaking ball in the dirt.

Last thing a catcher wants to see.

Down goes A.J. Pierzynski, doing his duty, making the catcher's instinctive move of throwing his body in front of the train.

Though the ball hits the dirt to his right, its tight spin redirects it on a crazy bounce back to the catcher's left. Uh-oh. Trouble. That ball could get loose. The Astros would score for the first time in forever.

But Pierzynski stops it. Not with his glove. Nor with his armor. And it's not like he makes a skilled workman's decision. He uses the meat of his left forearm. The ball hops so high his forearm just gets in its way. Fine. Catchers don't get style points. They get paid to stop 'em any way they can stop 'em.

Then Garcia strikes out the hitter who had a home run and double the night before. The Astros never score. Two hours later, the world championship trophy goes around the clamorous White Sox clubhouse. It's held high for all to see. It glitters in the TV lights. It glistens with champagne spray. And what A.J. Pierzynski did with that breaking ball in the dirt becomes more evidence that baseball's big deals happen only if you do the little deals first.

That little play became symbolic of the White Sox year. They showed that the ultimate answer is not money. Certainly, rich teams have the same advantage they've had for 101 years of the World Series. But the White Sox won with baseball's 13th highest payroll, middle-class spenders celebrating. Meanwhile, the megabucks Yankees and Red Sox wonder, "Scott Podsednik? Joe Crede? Willie Harris?"

For that matter, my notebook from Game 3 has this note: "Blum? G-e-o-f-f." He became a World Series hero a minute after being an anonymity. As to how that happened, A.J. Pierzynski said he knew. In the 13th inning, he went to Blum in the dugout. It was Blum's first World Series game, his first at-bat coming up in the 14th.

So the catcher made note of the fun the Astros have with their "Killer B's": Biggio, Bagwell, Berkman. And told Blum, "Don't be afraid. You're one of the 'Killer B's.' This is your ballpark. Hit a home run and win the game."

With two out, nobody on, Blum did it. His line drive over the right field wall started the Sox to the 7-5 victory that left the Astros moribund, the coup de grace delivered the next night when Garcia pitched seven masterful innings in a 1-0 classic.

Hmmm. "Classic"? After the Astros scored in the eighth inning of Game 3, they didn't score again all season. They sent 65 hitters to the plate. They had 25 different baserunners. They had 19 at-bats with runners on second and/or third. Nada. "Classic" may be a stretch. Maybe Freddy Garcia was less than masterful. Maybe the "Killer B's" simply lost their stingers somewhere.

Still, the White Sox were a delight, baseball players playing country hardball. Who couldn't root for a motley crew of Podsednik, Konerko, Iguchi and Uribe, Crede and Jenks? You had to love the manager, Ozzie Guillen. He stood near the batting cage before the last game, the biggest game of his career, and talked passionately about– what else?–the relative virtues of his fellow Venezuelan shortstop, Luis Aparicio, and today's god, Alex Rodriguez. Told that Rodriguez made the all-time Latino Legends team, Guillen all but levitated as he shouted, "A-Rod can't hold Aparicio's jock!"

And A.J. Pierzynski. Yapper, agitator, damn-the-torpedoes guy that you love on your team, hate on theirs. Guided his pitchers through mine fields. Started the late rally that assured victory in Game 1. "You gotta get my dad," Oswaldo Guillen said afterward, handing the catcher a bottle of champagne, and A.J. Pierzynski poured the sweet stuff onto Ozzie Guillen's head.

There was a red welt on the catcher's left forearm.

From the Freddy Garcia breaking ball.

Someone asked, "That hurt?"

"I," said A.J. Pierzynski, bringing champagne to his lips, shouting into the cacophony of World Series joy, "am feeling no pain."

It has been a very good year for A.J. Pierzynski, who can celebrate a World Series championship with wife Lisa and a new baby.

WORLD SERIES 137

2005 Game-by-Game Log
Home games shaded

GAME 1   April 4   White Sox 1, Indians 0   1-0
Buehrle retires the first 12 batters and allows only two hits over eight innings. Konerko is 2-for-3 in the Sox's first season-opening home game since 1990.

GAME 2   April 6   White Sox 4, Indians 3   2-0
Back-to-back homers by Konerko and Dye off closer Bob Wickman key a three-run rally in the ninth. Uribe's sacrifice fly produces the winning run.

GAME 3   April 7   Indians 11, White Sox 5 (11)   2-1
After Takatsu blows his first save opportunity, the Indians rally for six runs in the 11th off Vizcaino. Pierzynski hits his first Sox home run.

GAME 4   April 8   White Sox 5, Twins 1   3-1
Hernandez, who allows one run and six hits in seven innings and retires 11 of the final 12 batters he faces, wins his White Sox debut.

GAME 5   April 9   White Sox 8, Twins 5   4-1
Everett, Perez and Konerko hit home runs to give Garland, who is battling the flu, a nice cushion. Garland wins despite allowing 10 hits in six innings.

GAME 6   April 10   Twins 5, White Sox 2   4-2
Johan Santana continues his mastery of the Sox, striking out 11 in seven innings. Buehrle allows five runs and suffers his first loss.

GAME 7   April 11   White Sox 2, Indians 1   5-2
Garcia allows one run in eight innings and ruins the Indians' home opener. Podsednik drives in the game-winner in the seventh.

GAME 8   April 13   White Sox 5, Indians 4 (10)   6-2
Uribe hits his second game-deciding sacrifice fly in the 10th inning, and Hermanson records his first American League save.

GAME 9   April 14   Indians 8, White Sox 6   6-3
Hernandez allows four runs in the first inning, six (four earned) in five innings overall, and takes his first loss.

GAME 10   April 15   White Sox 6, Mariners 4   7-3
After Garland takes a perfect game into the seventh, the Sox have to hold off a rally. Uribe goes 2-for-3 with a homer and four RBIs.

GAME 11   April 16   White Sox 2, Mariners 1   8-3
Buehrle strikes out a career-high 12 in his 1-hour, 39-minute masterpiece. Konerko provides all the support he needs with two home runs.

GAME 12   April 17   Mariners 5, White Sox 4   8-4
Harris, trying to steal second base with two out in the ninth inning, gets thrown out by former Sox catcher Miguel Olivo. Garcia suffers the loss.

GAME 13   April 18   White Sox 5, Twins 4   9-4
Everett hits two homers, including a two-run tiebreaker in the sixth, as the Sox rally from a 3-1 deficit. Crede also homers for Chicago.

GAME 14   April 19   White Sox 3, Twins 1   10-4
Hernandez allows 10 hits in six scoreless innings as the struggling Twins strand 12 baserunners.

GAME 15   April 20   White Sox 9, Tigers 1   11-4
Garland allows one run in eight innings, giving him three straight wins for the first time since 2003. Dye and Crede combine for seven RBIs.

GAME 16   April 21   White Sox 4, Tigers 3   12-4
Podsednik's two-run, seventh-inning single helps the Sox overcome a 3-1 deficit. Crede extends his hitting streak to a career-high 12 games.

GAME 17   April 22   White Sox 8, Royals 2   13-4
Garcia retires 12 straight batters from the third to seventh innings en route to victory. Podsednik's three stolen bases ignite the offense.

GAME 18   April 23   White Sox 3, Royals 2 (10)   14-4
Rowand's 10th-inning hit scores the winner and gives the Sox their best-ever 18-game start. But a hamstring strain sidelines Contreras after 3⅓ innings.

GAME 19   April 24   White Sox 4, Royals 3   15-4
Four errors and two-hit pitching by the Royals through seven innings can't stop the Sox. They win on Ozuna's pinch-hit double in the eighth.

GAME 20   April 25   White Sox 6, Athletics 0   16-4
Garland pitches a four-hit shutout and Widger hits his first home run since 2000. The Sox's winning streak stretches to eight games.

GAME 21   April 26   Athletics 9, White Sox 7   16-5
Dye drops a routine fly in the eighth inning, opening the door for a winning streak-ending rally. Buehrle gives up seven runs in six innings.

GAME 22   April 27   Athletics 2, White Sox 1   16-6
Marco Scutaro's ninth-inning single decides the issue. Guillen gets ejected after arguing that Crede was hit by a pitch in the top of the frame.

GAME 23   April 29   Tigers 3, White Sox 2 (11)   16-7
Nook Logan's 11th-inning triple off Takatsu scores the winner, after Rowand ties it with a sacrifice fly off closer Troy Percival. The Sox strand 16 runners.

GAME 24   April 30   White Sox 4, Tigers 3   17-7
Iguchi's three-run single caps another comeback win and gives the Sox their franchise record-tying 17th victory in April.

GAME 25   May 1   White Sox 8, Tigers 0   18-7
Garland pitches his second straight four-hit shutout, only the third shutout of his career, and becomes the A.L.'s first five-game winner.

MAY 1: Jon Garland, en route to a win over the Tigers and his second straight shutout.

GAME 26 — May 3 — White Sox 5, Royals 4 — 19-7
Iguchi goes 4-for-4 and hits his first major league home run. But Everett's two-run double in the eighth makes a winner out of Buehrle.

GAME 27 — May 4 — White Sox 4, Royals 2 — 20-7
Despite being outhit 9-6, the Sox and Garcia win. Hermanson turns heads by earning his fourth save with 1 2/3 scoreless innings.

GAME 28 — May 5 — White Sox 2, Royals 1 — 21-7
The Royals give one away, issuing three straight eighth-inning walks that score the tying and winning runs. Contreras benefits from the generosity.

GAME 29 — May 6 — White Sox 5, Blue Jays 3 — 22-7
Pierzynski's two-run single in the eighth ends his 2-for-29 career slump in Toronto and helps Hernandez improve to 4-1.

GAME 30 — May 7 — White Sox 10, Blue Jays 7 — 23-7
Konerko homers twice and drives in five runs a day after ending an 0-for-26 skid. Garland is shaky, but stretches his winning streak to eight games.

GAME 31 — May 8 — White Sox 5, Blue Jays 4 — 24-7
Buehrle allows four runs (two earned) in 7 1/3 innings to win his fourth straight decision. Dye and Uribe help his cause with home runs.

GAME 32 — May 9 — Devil Rays 4, White Sox 2 — 24-8
Chris Singleton's two RBIs help end his former team's eight-game winning streak. Sox bats go silent after a two-run first inning.

GAME 33 — May 10 — Devil Rays 7, White Sox 6 — 24-9
Takatsu surrenders a one-out walkoff homer to Jorge Cantu in the ninth inning. The Sox's 7-through-9 hitters go a combined 7-for-11.

GAME 34 — May 11 — White Sox 5, Devil Rays 2 — 25-9
The Sox avoid being swept by the lowly Devil Rays, thanks to a strong effort from Hernandez. Hermanson is strong over the final 1 2/3 innings.

GAME 35 — May 12 — White Sox 3, Orioles 2 — 26-9
Garland pitches eight innings and becomes the first Sox starter to open a season 7-0 since James Baldwin in 2000. Konerko appears in 1,000th game.

GAME 36 — May 13 — White Sox 5, Orioles 3 — 27-9
Konerko's broken-bat single in the seventh caps a rally from a three-run hole. Everett's RBI single snaps a 1-for-18 pinch-hit skid.

GAME 37 — May 14 — Orioles 9, White Sox 6 — 27-10
An early three-run lead vanishes as the Sox are outscored, 7-1, in the final six innings. Garcia yields seven runs, the most by a Sox starter to date.

GAME 38 — May 15 — Orioles 6, White Sox 2 — 27-11
The Sox, who had led in each of their first 37 games (a major league record), trail all the way in this one as Erik Bedard allows five hits in seven innings.

GAME 39 — May 16 — Rangers 7, White Sox 6 — 27-12
Kevin Mench's second home run, a solo shot in the ninth inning off Marte, secures a win for the Rangers. Hernandez lasts just 2 2/3 innings.

GAME 40 — May 17 — White Sox 5, Rangers 2 — 28-12
Garland becomes the first Sox pitcher since John Whitehead in 1935 to win his first eight starts of a season. Hermanson's scoreless-innings streak hits 19.

GAME 41 — May 18 — White Sox 7, Rangers 0 — 29-12
Buehrle combines with Politte and Cotts on a nine-hit shutout. Pierzynski hits a home run for the fourth consecutive game.

GAME 42 — May 20 — White Sox 5, Cubs 1 — 30-12
Garcia outduels Greg Maddux, and Pierzynski and Dye combine for five of the Sox's 10 hits in their first win at Wrigley Field since 2003.

GAME 43 — May 21 — White Sox 5, Cubs 3 — 31-12
Konerko's two-run, line-drive single, just in front of diving center fielder Corey Patterson, keys a four-run inning that gives Contreras a win.

GAME 44 — May 22 — Cubs 4, White Sox 3 — 31-13
McCarthy, filling in for an injured Hernandez, allows two runs in 5 1/3 innings of his major league debut, but the Cubs rally against Vizcaino.

GAME 45 — May 23 — Angels 4, White Sox 0 — 31-14
Garland's 10-game winning streak ends, thanks to the five-hit pitching of Ervin Santana–a 22-year-old making his second big-league start.

GAME 46 — May 24 — White Sox 2, Angels 1 (11) — 32-14
Iguchi's 11th-inning single drives in the winning run, giving Marte a victory. Buehrle allows only four hits in nine brisk innings.

GAME 47 — May 25 — White Sox 4, Angels 2 — 33-14
Garcia allows only two runs in seven innings and is backed by Konerko and Widger home runs. Garcia goes to 11-2 over his last 14 road starts.

GAME 48 — May 26 — Angels 3, White Sox 2 — 33-15
Rookie Dallas McPherson hits a two-run, seventh-inning homer off Contreras, who takes the loss despite recording nine strikeouts.

GAME 49 — May 27 — Rangers 6, White Sox 2 — 33-16
Alfonso Soriano hits two of the Rangers' four home runs off McCarthy, who allows six runs over five innings in his second major league start.

GAME 50 — May 29 — Rangers 12, White Sox 4 — 33-17
The honeymoon is over for Garland, who allows seven runs in his second straight loss after opening 8-0. Texas wins its eighth straight game.

2005 Game-by-Game Log continued

| GAME 51 | May 30 | White Sox 5, Angels 4 | 34-17 |

Perez hits a two-run, game-ending single off Scot Shields, giving Politte his first win since April 2003. Frank Thomas is 0-for-2 in his 2005 debut.

| GAME 52 | May 31 | White Sox 5, Angels 4 | 35-17 |

Dye hits the 28th walkoff home run in U.S. Cellular Field history, giving Politte his second win in as many nights. He works 1⅔ innings.

| GAME 53 | June 1 | Angels 10, White Sox 7 | 35-18 |

Two four-run innings allow the Angels to steal one from the Sox, who watch their bullpen surrender six runs over the last three frames.

| GAME 54 | June 3 | White Sox 6, Indians 4 | 36-18 |

Hernandez, making his first start since May 16, hits four batters but still earns a victory. Chicago's four-run first helps his cause.

| GAME 55 | June 4 | White Sox 6, Indians 5 | 37-18 |

Garland, 5-0 at home, wins his ninth game and the Sox post their 18th one-run victory. Konerko and Crede homer as the Sox win their 14th series.

| GAME 56 | June 5 | Indians 6, White Sox 4 (12) | 37-19 |

Thomas' first home run since June 22, 2004–a solo shot in the 10th–is wasted when Hermanson yields two runs during a sloppy 12th inning.

| GAME 57 | June 6 | White Sox 9, Rockies 3 | 38-19 |

After allowing three runs in the first, Garcia retires the final 22 batters he faces. Pierzynski's two-run double keys a three-run fifth.

| GAME 58 | June 7 | White Sox 2, Rockies 1 | 39-19 |

RBI singles by Dye and Pierzynski decide a low-scoring game at Coors Field. Cotts strikes out four in a strong two-inning relief effort.

| GAME 59 | June 8 | White Sox 15, Rockies 5 | 40-19 |

Three RBIs apiece by Uribe and Everett help Hernandez win his sixth straight decision. The Sox rally for 10 runs in the eighth and ninth innings.

| GAME 60 | June 10 | White Sox 4, Padres 2 | 41-19 |

Garland becomes the A.L.'s first 10-game winner and gets his first career RBI. Hermanson stretches his saves streak to 15.

| GAME 61 | June 11 | Padres 2, White Sox 1 | 41-20 |

Hermanson blows his first save as the Padres rally for two in the ninth. A first-and-third threat in the eighth ends with three straight Sox strikeouts.

| GAME 62 | June 12 | White Sox 8, Padres 5 | 42-20 |

Rowand's three-run homer off closer Trevor Hoffman secures a 5-1 trip against the N.L. West. Cotts, Vizcaino and Politte combine for four scoreless innings.

| GAME 63 | June 13 | Diamondbacks 8, White Sox 1 | 42-21 |

Four home runs and a six-run second inning doom Contreras as the Diamondbacks win their first game at U.S. Cellular Field.

| GAME 64 | June 14 | Diamondbacks 10, White Sox 4 | 42-22 |

Konerko, Everett and Dye homers provide little consolation for Hernandez, who is pounded and sees his six-game win streak come to an ugly end.

| GAME 65 | June 15 | White Sox 12, Diamondbacks 6 | 43-22 |

The Sox score 10 runs in the sixth–their biggest inning in five years–thanks in large part to home runs by Thomas, Uribe and Konerko.

| GAME 66 | June 17 | White Sox 6, Dodgers 0 | 44-22 |

Buehrle's eight-hit shutout highlights the Sox's first game against the Dodgers since the 1959 World Series. Thomas and Dye hit home runs.

| GAME 67 | June 18 | White Sox 5, Dodgers 3 | 45-22 |

Pierzynski's first career walkoff homer, a two-run shot, caps a four-run ninth inning. Garcia works eight innings after a 40-pitch first.

| GAME 68 | June 19 | White Sox 4, Dodgers 3 | 46-22 |

The Sox rally late against the Dodgers for a second straight night, this time winning on Rowand's two-run, eighth-inning single.

JULY 24: Ending a long slump, Tadahito Iguchi drives in three runs in a win over Boston.

| GAME 69 | June 20 | White Sox 11, Royals 8 | 47-22 |

Thomas, Konerko and Dye hit homers, but Pierzynski's two-run bloop single is the difference-maker. The Sox stretch their winning streak to five.

| GAME 70 | June 21 | White Sox 5, Royals 1 | 48-22 |

Fans shower Guillen with boos when he removes Garland with one out in the ninth. Podsednik goes 3-for-4 as the Sox get 10 hits, all singles.

| GAME 71 | June 22 | White Sox 5, Royals 1 | 49-22 |

Buehrle's winning streak reaches a career-high eight games, but his score-less-innings streak is snapped at 25 by an unearned run in the eighth.

| GAME 72 | June 24 | White Sox 12, Cubs 2 | 50-22 |

Homers by Thomas, Crede and Pierzynski make life easy for Garcia, who works seven innings and helps the Sox stretch their win streak to eight.

| GAME 73 | June 25 | Cubs 6, White Sox 2 | 50-23 |

Greg Maddux keeps Sox hitters off-balance, Aramis Ramirez hits a first-inning grand slam off Contreras and the Cubs end the Sox's winning streak.

| GAME 74 | June 26 | Cubs 2, White Sox 0 | 50-24 |

Mark Prior and two relievers shut down the Sox and Garland as the Cubs even the season interleague matchup at three games apiece.

| GAME 75 | June 28 | White Sox 2, Tigers 1 | 51-24 |

Buehrle outduels Nate Robertson, Dye snaps a 1-1 tie with a homer in the sixth and Hermanson survives a leadoff ninth-inning triple for his 18th save.

| GAME 76 | June 29 | White Sox 4, Tigers 3 (13) | 52-24 |

A strong showing by the bullpen pays off as Thomas delivers a leadoff homer in the 13th inning. A Konerko homer gives him 12 RBIs in 13 games.

140 THE PRIDE OF CHICAGO

| GAME 77 | June 30 | White Sox 6, Tigers 1 | 53-24 |

After a 2-hour, 4-minute rain delay, Garcia allows five hits in his first complete game. Homers by Crede and Everett supply five of the six runs.

| GAME 78 | July 1 | Athletics 6, White Sox 2 | 53-25 |

Contreras throws three wild pitches and walks seven batters, tying a career high. Two of the A's runs score on walks, another on a wild pitch.

| GAME 79 | July 2 | White Sox 5, Athletics 3 | 54-25 |

Working through several middle-inning jams, Garland hangs on for his career-high 13th win. Crede breaks a tie with his homer in the eighth.

| GAME 80 | July 3 | Athletics 7, White Sox 2 | 54-26 |

The A's score four runs in the sixth and hand Buehrle (10-2) his first loss since April 10. Thomas and Dye hit homers in a losing cause.

| GAME 81 | July 4 | White Sox 10, Devil Rays 8 | 55-26 |

Dye's Fourth of July explosion nets a career-high six RBIs on a grand slam and two-run single. The Sox reach the halfway point with baseball's best record.

| GAME 82 | July 5 | White Sox 6, Devil Rays 4 | 56-26 |

Thomas' three-run homer in the eighth inning lifts the Sox a whopping 30 games over .500. The Big Hurt now has 18 RBIs in his first 69 at-bats.

| GAME 83 | July 6 | White Sox 7, Devil Rays 2 | 57-26 |

Contreras, winless for a month and his starting job in danger, finally earns a victory as Thomas continues his torrid hitting with a three-run homer.

| GAME 84 | July 8 | Athletics 4, White Sox 2 | 57-27 |

Garland allows eight hits, throws 112 pitches and is chased after five innings—his shortest start of the season. Podsednik's two steals give him 43.

| GAME 85 | July 9 | Athletics 10, White Sox 1 | 57-28 |

Barry Zito holds the Sox to two hits in seven innings. Ozuna's second error sparks a three-run seventh inning, blowing open a 2-1 A's lead.

| GAME 86 | July 10 | Athletics 9, White Sox 8 (11) | 57-29 |

The A's become the first team to complete a three-game sweep of the Sox when Nick Swisher delivers an 11th-inning double. Konerko gets five hits.

| GAME 87 | July 14 | White Sox 1, Indians 0 | 58-29 |

Hounded by trade rumors, Contreras allows three hits in seven innings to start a second-half rebound. He's 2-0 with a 1.83 ERA in five starts vs. the Indians.

| GAME 88 | July 15 | White Sox 7, Indians 1 | 59-29 |

Ozuna and Widger make the most of starting opportunities, going 7-for-9. A four-run first against C.C. Sabathia gives Garcia plenty of breathing room.

| GAME 89 | July 16 | White Sox 7, Indians 5 | 60-29 |

In his first start since the All-Star Game, an erratic Buehrle hits Travis Hafner in the mouth with a pitch. He labors through seven and gets his 11th win.

| GAME 90 | July 17 | White Sox 4, Indians 0 | 61-29 |

Iguchi and Pierzynski homer, Garland pitches six strong innings and the Sox complete their first four-game sweep at Cleveland in 42 years.

| GAME 91 | July 18 | White Sox 7, Tigers 5 | 62-29 |

Battling a sore back, Crede hits a three-run homer during a five-run, three-homer rally in the seventh. The Sox lift their A.L. Central record to 31-5.

| GAME 92 | July 19 | Tigers 7, White Sox 1 | 62-30 |

Contreras takes an ugly loss as the Tigers score all seven runs with two out. Jeremy Bonderman allows three hits in eight innings.

| GAME 93 | July 20 | Tigers 8, White Sox 6 | 62-31 |

Too little too late: A three-run ninth can't rescue Garcia's six-game winning streak. Injuries sideline Podsednik and Crede.

| GAME 94 | July 21 | Red Sox 6, White Sox 5 | 62-32 |

When Crede drops a ninth-inning foul pop, Manny Ramirez takes advantage of his second chance and hits a one-out homer to snap a 5-5 tie.

| GAME 95 | July 22 | White Sox 8, Red Sox 4 | 63-32 |

Pierzynski and Uribe hit two-out, three-run homers off Tim Wakefield in the sixth inning, and Garland becomes baseball's first 15-game winner.

| GAME 96 | July 23 | Red Sox 3, White Sox 0 | 63-33 |

Wade Miller works seven scoreless innings for his first win since May 30. Hernandez gets burned by Ramirez's two-run homer in the first.

| GAME 97 | July 24 | White Sox 6, Red Sox 4 | 64-33 |

Iguchi, mired in a 3-for-17 slump, goes 3-for-4, hits a homer and drives in three runs to make a winner out of Contreras.

| GAME 98 | July 25 | White Sox 14, Royals 6 | 65-33 |

After missing four games because of spider bites, Dye gets three hits and four RBIs to pace a 22-hit attack. Podsednik improves to 14-of-14 stealing third.

| GAME 99 | July 26 | Royals 7, White Sox 1 | 65-34 |

Mike Sweeney's bunt single is the shocker in a six-run sixth. Three errors—two by Uribe—help the Royals snap an 11-game skid vs. the Sox.

| GAME 100 | July 27 | Royals 6, White Sox 5 (13) | 65-35 |

Emil Brown's run-scoring single caps a 13th-inning rally against Vizcaino. Garland leaves with a 5-2 lead but the bullpen can't protect his 16th win.

| GAME 101 | July 29 | White Sox 7, Orioles 2 | 66-35 |

El Duque gets his first win in more than seven weeks, thanks to the three-RBI efforts of Konerko and Everett (both of whom hit home runs).

| GAME 102 | July 30 | White Sox 9, Orioles 6 | 67-35 |

Pierzynski and Dye hit consecutive home runs in a four-run eighth as the Sox rally from a 6-4 deficit and drop the Orioles two games below .500.

| GAME 103 | July 31 | White Sox 9, Orioles 4 | 68-35 |

A five-run first gives Garcia all the support and confidence he needs after going 0-4 with a 5.54 ERA in his last four starts against the O's.

| GAME 104 | August 1 | White Sox 6, Orioles 3 | 69-35 |

Buehrle's streak of pitching at least six innings ends at 49 games after he is ejected for hitting B.J. Surhoff. He still gets his 12th victory.

| GAME 105 | August 2 | Blue Jays 7, White Sox 3 | 69-36 |

Rookie Russ Adams hits two homers off Garland and the Sox see their four-game winning streak end. Josh Towers wins for just the third time in 14 starts.

| GAME 106 | August 3 | Blue Jays 4, White Sox 3 | 69-37 |

Gregg Zaun's three-run double caps a four-run first against Hernandez. The Sox strand nine and go 0-for-11 with runners in scoring position.

| GAME 107 | August 4 | White Sox 5, Blue Jays 4 | 70-37 |

Iguchi's tiebreaking home run in the eighth inning helps the Sox avoid a sweep. Contreras doesn't allow an earned run in his five innings.

| GAME 108 | August 5 | Mariners 4, White Sox 2 | 70-38 |

Unsafe at home: The Sox lose for the 10th time in 14 games at U.S. Cellular, even though Rowand and Pierzynski hit home runs.

| GAME 109 | August 6 | White Sox 4, Mariners 2 | 71-38 |

Konerko's 26th home run is one of four White Sox hits—enough for Buehrle to prevail in a pitching duel with Jamie Moyer.

| GAME 110 | August 7 | White Sox 3, Mariners 1 | 72-38 |

A great catch by center fielder Rowand as he crashes into the wall robs Richie Sexson and ends an eighth-inning rally. Garland picks up his 16th win.

| GAME 111 | August 8 | Yankees 3, White Sox 2 | 72-39 |

A two-run, first-inning homer by Alex Rodriguez welcomes El Duque back to New York. Sox come up short against Mike Mussina and three relievers.

| GAME 112 | August 9 | White Sox 2, Yankees 1 | 73-39 |

Ignoring the distraction of a fan falling from the upper deck into the net behind home plate, the Sox roll on homers by Konerko and Iguchi.

2005 Game-by-Game Log *continued*

GAME 113   August 10   White Sox 2, Yankees 1 (10)   74-39
With one out in the 10th, Uribe triples against Mariano Rivera and scores the winning run on Podsednik's grounder, barely beating the throw home.

GAME 114   August 12   Red Sox 9, White Sox 8   74-40
David Ortiz drives in a career-high six runs as the Red Sox beat up on Buehrle, who yields more than five runs for only the third time in 24 starts.

GAME 115   August 13   Red Sox 7, White Sox 4   74-41
Tony Graffanino punishes his former team with three hits, and knuckleballer Tim Wakefield takes care of the rest. Garland yields five runs in 5⅓ innings.

GAME 116   August 15   Twins 4, White Sox 2   74-42
Contreras gets battered for four runs and four hits in the fourth inning. It will be Contreras' last poor outing of the regular season.

GAME 117   August 16   Twins 9, White Sox 4 (16)   74-43
In the longest game ever played at U.S. Cellular Field, the Twins score five runs in the 16th inning. Hermanson blows his second save in the ninth.

GAME 118   August 17   Twins 5, White Sox 1   74-44
Everett ends Johan Santana's no-hit bid with a leadoff single in the seventh, but the Sox don't score until Konerko's ninth-inning homer.

GAME 119   August 19   Yankees 3, White Sox 1   74-45
Mike Mussina outduels Garland as the Sox suffer their 14th loss in 20 home games. Konerko is scratched after hurting his back in batting practice.

GAME 120   August 20   Yankees 5, White Sox 0   74-46
The losing streak hits a season-high seven games. Hernandez commits his first two errors in 109 games and commits a balk in a strange outing.

GAME 121   August 21   White Sox 6, Yankees 2   75-46
Iguchi, Rowand and Konerko hit consecutive homers off Randy Johnson in the fourth. Widger adds a three-run shot later in the monster inning.

GAME 122   August 23   Twins 1, White Sox 0   75-47
Jacque Jones ends Garcia's no-hit bid with a leadoff homer in the eighth. Johan Santana holds the Sox to three hits over eight innings.

GAME 123   August 24   White Sox 6, Twins 4   76-47
Everett homers and drives in four runs and the Sox defense turns four double plays. Buehrle snaps a personal five-game skid vs. the Twins.

GAME 124   August 25   White Sox 2, Twins 1 (10)   77-47
Hermanson blows his third save in 34 chances, but Perez saves the day with a go-ahead single in the 10th inning. The Sox get back to 30 over .500.

GAME 125   August 26   White Sox 5, Mariners 3 (12)   78-47
Iguchi wins it with a two-run blast in the 12th, but rookie Brian Anderson is the star with two homers in only his fifth major league game.

GAME 126   August 27   White Sox 4, Mariners 3   79-47
Behind Contreras, the Sox win their first A.L. West Coast road series in five seasons. Dye matches his career best with a 4-for-4 effort.

GAME 127   August 28   Mariners 9, White Sox 2   79-48
Garcia yields a season-high eight runs in a rough return to Safeco Field. The former Mariner makes his shortest start of the season (4⅓ innings).

GAME 128   August 29   Rangers 7, White Sox 5   79-49
Iguchi's three errors, the most by one White Sox player since Jose Valentin on April 8, 2000, contributes to Chicago's 10th loss in 15 games.

GAME 129   August 30   Rangers 8, White Sox 6   79-50
In the opener of a doubleheader, Garland yields a pair of two-run homers to Mark Teixeira and leaves after 4⅓ innings–his shortest outing of the season.

GAME 130   August 30   White Sox 8, Rangers 0   80-50
McCarthy helps a struggling rotation with 7⅔ strong innings for his first major league win. Dye's two homers and six RBIs back up the rookie.

GAME 131   August 31   Rangers 9, White Sox 2   80-51
The Sox get another poor outing from Hernandez (six runs and six hits in five innings) and complete their first losing month of the season: 12-16.

GAME 132   Sept. 1   White Sox 12, Tigers 3   81-51
Contreras does not allow a walk for the third straight start and Pierzynski goes 3-for-3 with a homer and three RBIs. Every Sox batter gets a hit.

GAME 133   Sept. 2   White Sox 9, Tigers 1   82-51
Garcia wins for the first time since July 31 as Everett and Uribe hit three-run homers. The Tigers' only run scores on a wild pitch in the fourth.

GAME 134   Sept. 3   White Sox 6, Tigers 2   83-51
Iguchi, back in the lineup after attending to personal business for two days, singles, doubles and triples. The resurgent Sox win their third straight.

GAME 135   Sept. 4   White Sox 2, Tigers 0   84-51
Garland pitches his third shutout of the season and wins his 17th game as Konerko hits a solo homer, completing a four-game sweep of the Tigers.

GAME 136   Sept. 5   White Sox 5, Red Sox 3   85-51
McCarthy outduels Curt Schilling with seven shutout innings as the Sox make a successful one-day side trip to Boston to make up an August 14 rainout.

GAME 137   Sept. 6   White Sox 6, Royals 5   86-51
Hernandez wins for the first time since July 29. The Sox draw 14,571, the lowest home total since 12,712 watched the Royals play on May 4.

GAME 138   Sept. 7   White Sox 1, Royals 0   87-51
Konerko homers for the fourth straight game as the Sox move to a season-high 36 games over .500. They are 30-15 in one-run games.

GAME 139   Sept. 8   Royals 4, White Sox 2   87-52
Ozuna steals home in a two-run fifth inning, but the Royals rally for three runs in the sixth to snap the Sox's seven-game winning streak.

GAME 140   Sept. 9   Angels 6, White Sox 5 (12)   87-53
Vladimir Guerrero leads off the 12th with a double, then scores from second on Bengie Molina's bunt. He beats Iguchi's errant throw.

GAME 141   Sept. 10   Angels 10, White Sox 5   87-54
Garland allows seven runs and eight hits in six innings. Crede, just activated from the D.L., stops his 0-for-22 skid with a double and single.

GAME 142   Sept. 11   Angels 6, White Sox 1   87-55
Chone Figgins, Garret Anderson and Darin Erstad hit solo home runs off Hernandez in the first inning as the Angels complete a three-game sweep.

GAME 143   Sept. 13   White Sox 6, Royals 4   88-55
Two doubles lift Uribe's September average to a big league-high .487. Rowand gets four hits, including three doubles, as the Royals fall to 3-13 vs. the Sox.

GAME 144   Sept. 14   Royals 10, White Sox 9   88-56
Dye's error allows the third run to score in the ninth as Hermanson blows his fourth save. The loss and a sore back costs him his closer job.

GAME 145   Sept. 15   Royals 7, White Sox 5   88-57
Losing six of seven, including two straight to the worst team in baseball, prompts Guillen to say, "We flat-out stink." Buehrle is 5-5 in the second half.

GAME 146   Sept. 16   White Sox 2, Twins 1 (10)   89-57
Crede's infield single in the 10th breaks a 1-1 tie. Rookie Bobby Jenks retires all four batters he faces for his first major league victory.

GAME 147   Sept. 17   Twins 5, White Sox 0   89-58
Johan Santana fans 13 and improves to 6-0 with a 0.81 ERA in his last six starts against the Sox. Hernandez lasts 3⅔ innings and loses his starting job.

GAME 148   Sept. 18   White Sox 2, Twins 1   90-58
Contreras works eight innings for his sixth straight win. Second baseman Nick Punto misplays Dye's two-out grounder in the eighth for the go-ahead run.

142   THE PRIDE OF CHICAGO

AUGUST 21: Aaron Rowand hits the second of three consecutive home runs off Randy Johnson.

GAME 149	Sept. 19	Indians 7, White Sox 5	90-59

On his first day as closer, Jenks blows a save, yielding a two-run single to Aaron Boone in the eighth inning. The Central lead is down to 2½ games.

GAME 150	Sept. 20	White Sox 7, Indians 6 (10)	91-59

Crede hits the biggest home run of his career leading off the 10th inning. Crede also opens the scoring for the Sox with a two-run shot in the third.

GAME 151	Sept. 21	Indians 8, White Sox 0	91-60

Travis Hafner continues to beat up on the Sox, blasting two home runs to back up Scott Elarton's five-hitter. Garland's slide continues.

GAME 152	Sept. 22	Twins 4, White Sox 1 (11)	91-61

The Twins score three in the 11th and the Central lead slips to 1½—the smallest margin since May 1. The Sox waste a bases-loaded threat in the ninth.

GAME 153	Sept. 23	White Sox 3, Twins 1	92-61

Contreras continues to carry the rotation, holding the Twins to six hits in his first career complete game. Everett drops from third to sixth in the lineup.

GAME 154	Sept. 24	White Sox 8, Twins 1	93-61

Dye hits a three-run homer for the second straight game and Garcia works eight strong innings. The consecutive wins are the first since September 6-7.

GAME 155	Sept. 25	White Sox 4, Twins 1	94-61

In the regular-season home finale, Buehrle shows up big with a complete-game four-hitter and Konerko belts his first homer since September 9.

GAME 156	Sept. 26	Tigers 4, White Sox 3	94-62

With the Indians idle, the Sox blow key scoring chances and pay for it in the ninth when South Side native Curtis Granderson hits a walkoff homer.

GAME 157	Sept. 27	Tigers 3, White Sox 2	94-63

Crede, the team's hottest hitter, leaves to attend the birth of his second child. His absence is felt as the Sox strand 12 runners.

GAME 158	Sept. 28	White Sox 8, Tigers 2	95-63

Contreras, solidifying his status as the No. 1 starter in the playoffs, wins his eighth straight start as the Sox break out of their offensive doldrums.

GAME 159	Sept. 29	White Sox 4, Tigers 2	96-63

Konerko hits his 40th home run and Garcia pitches seven strong innings as the relieved Sox clinch their first A.L. Central crown since 2000.

GAME 160	Sept. 30	White Sox 3, Indians 2	97-63

Called scrubs by a radio reporter before the game, the backup Sox flex their muscle. Jenks throws his first 1-2-3 inning since being named closer.

GAME 161	October 1	White Sox 4, Indians 3	98-63

Iguchi's three-run homer highlights a four-run seventh inning. Garland looks solid as the Sox improve to 9-0 in one-run games against the Indians.

GAME 162	October 2	White Sox 3, Indians 1	99-63

McCarthy continues to dazzle as the Indians' wild-card hopes are dashed. The Sox get 99 victories for the first time since 1983.

GAME-BY-GAME LOG 143

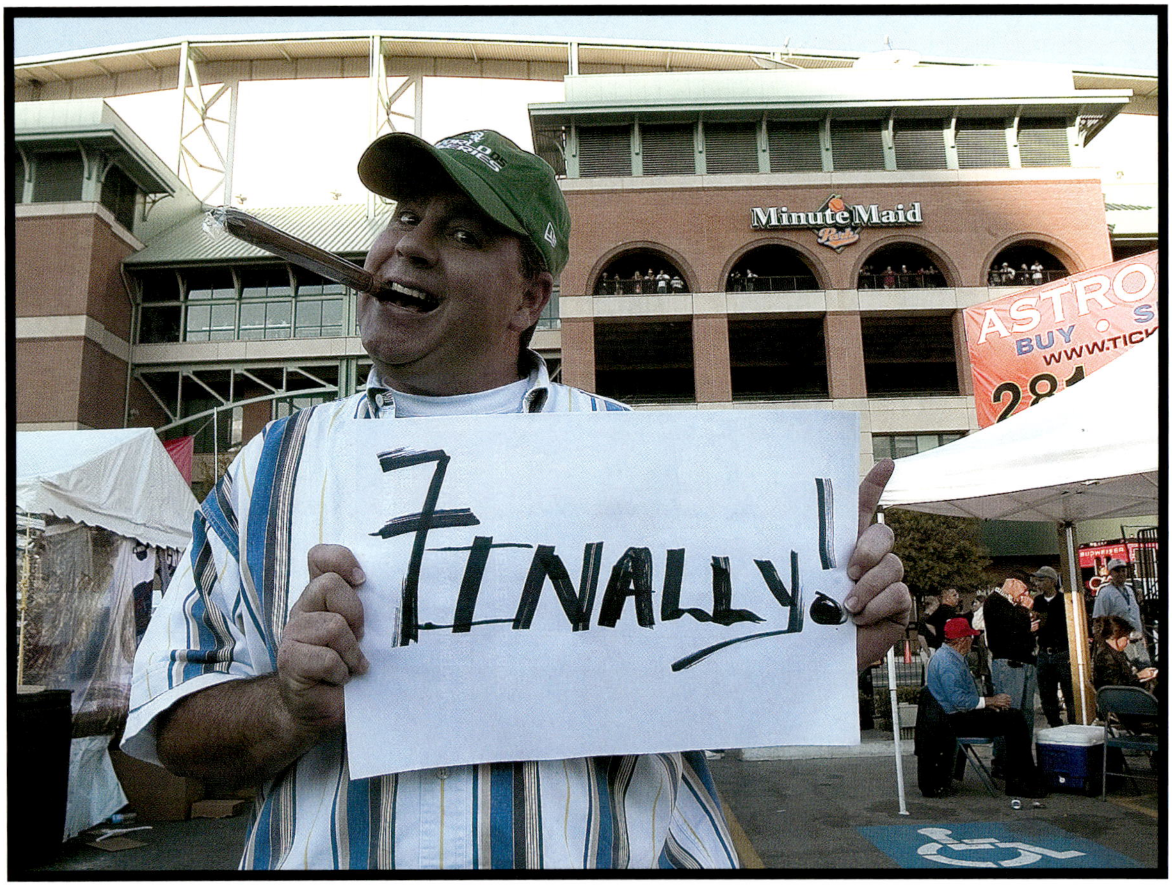
Minute Maid
FINALLY!